FUNDAMENTALS OF
ORIGAMIC ARCHITECTURE

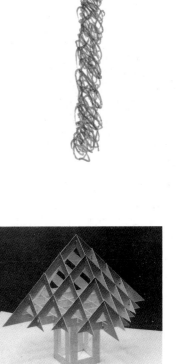

MESSAGE FROM THE AUTHOR

Greeting cards that feature folded and cut paper have become a popular artform both within and outside exhibitions. After publishing these books, it is gratifying to see that there are so many aficionados of this art. This is the seventh volume in the Pop-up Paper Craft Series and I have done my best to make this the most enjoyable. Due to great demand, the previous volumes have already been translated into English, German, Dutch and Danish. I truly hope that you will enjoy this book as well, and that it will find interested readers for another hundred years. This book is co-authored by Ms. Keiko Nakazawa, who is also very busy creating Origamic Art.

MASAHIRO CHATANI

Author: Masahiro Chatani
1934: Born in Hiroshima
1956: Graduated: Tokyo Institute of Technology
1961: Researcher for the Ministry of Construction
1969: Assistant Professor, Tokyo Institute of Technology
1977: Visiting Associate Professor, University of Washington at Seattle
1980-: Professor, Tokyo Institute of Technology

Co-Author: Keiko Nakazawa
Born in Nagoya, Japan,
Graduated Shukutoku High School
Licensed Japanese Dance Teacher
Opened Private School
1983: Studied Origamic Architecture

Translated
by
Chieko Willemsen
Matt Willemsen

★Published by ONDORISHA PUBLISHERS, LTD.,
  11-11 Nishigoken-cho, shinjuku-ku, Tokyo 162, Japan.
★Sole Overseas Distributor: Japan Publications Trading CO Ltd.
  P. O. Box 5030 Tokyo International, Tokyo, Japan.
★Distributed
· in United States by Kodansha America, INC.
  114 Fifth Avenue, New York, NY 10011, U.S.A.
· in Canada by Fitzhenry & Writeside LTD.
  195 Allstate Parkway, Markham, Ontario L3R 4T8, Canada.
· in British Isles & European Continent by Premier Book Marketing Ltd.,
  1 Gower Street, London WCIE 6HA, England.
· in Australia by Bookwise International.
  54 Crittenden Road, Findon, South Australia 5023, Australia.
· in The Far East and Japan by Japan Publications Trading Co, Ltd.,
  1-2-1, Sarugaku-cho, Chiyoda-ku, Tokyo 101, Japan

10 9 8 7 6 5 4 3 2 1

ISBN 0-87040-943-3
Printed in Singapore

ONDORI

POP-UP GEOMETRIC ORIGAMI

ORIGAMIC ARCHITECTURE
BY
MASAHIRO CHATANI
KEIKO NAKAZAWA

GEOMETRIC ORIGAMI

CONTENTS

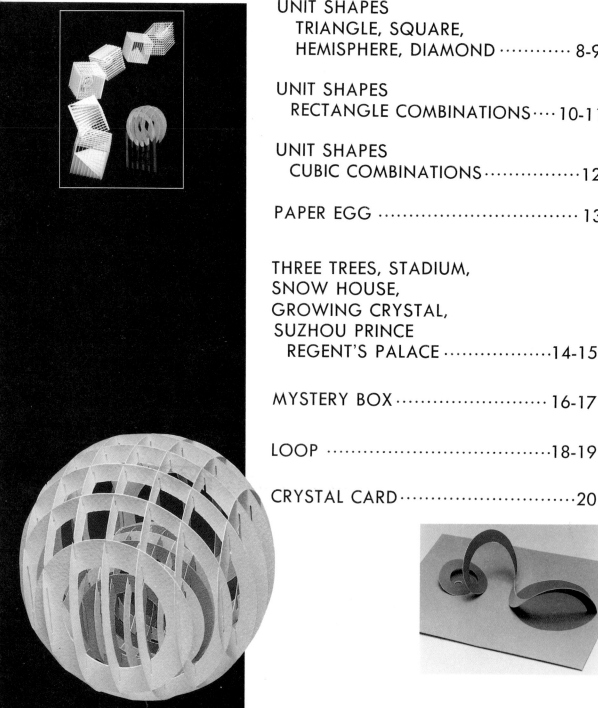

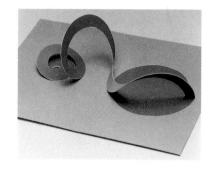

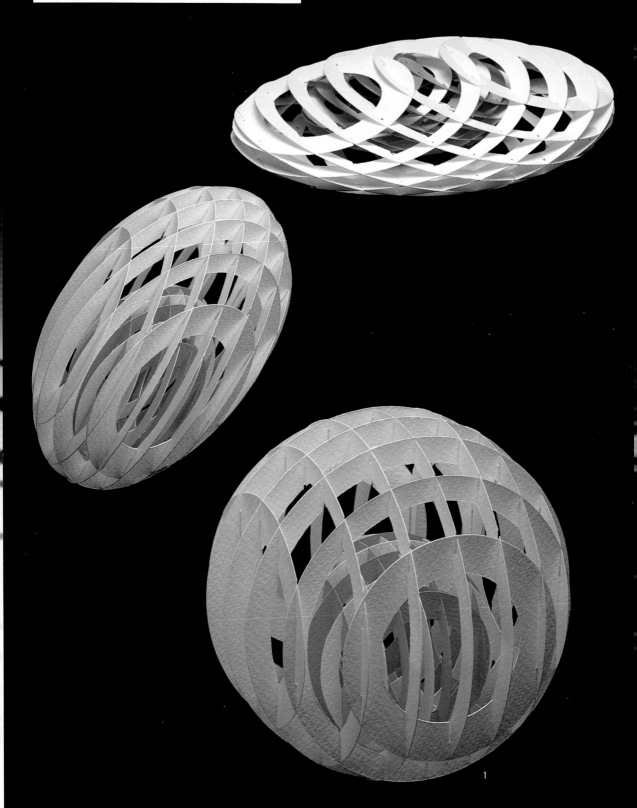

1

Actual-size pattern for ① on page 36

COMBINATION SHAPES

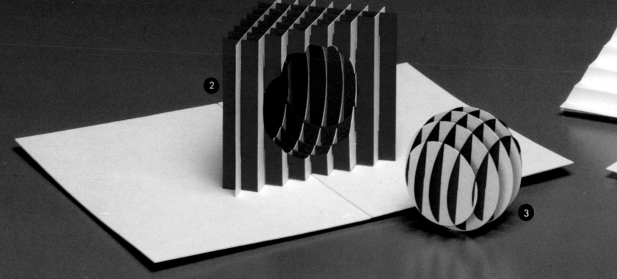

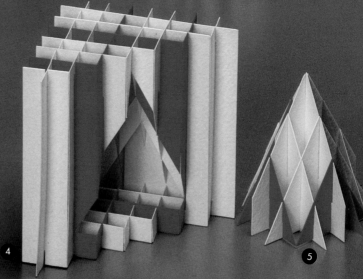

Actual-size pattern for ② on page 23
Actual-size pattern for ③ on page 23
Actual-size pattern for ④ on page 56
Actual-size pattern for ⑤ on page 56

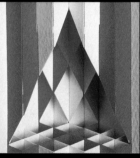

Actual-size pattern for ⑥ on page 51
Actual-size pattern for ⑦ on page 51
Actual-size pattern for ⑧ on page 58
Actual-size pattern for ⑨ on page 58

⑩

⑪

Actual-size pattern for ⑩ on page 40
Actual-size pattern for ⑪ on page 42

Actual-size pattern for ⑫ on page 41
Actual-size pattern for ⑬ on page 42

UNIT SHAPES RECTANGLE COMBINATIONS

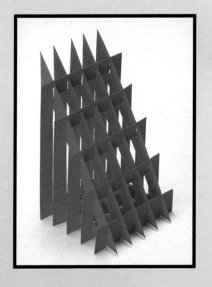

Actual-size pattern for ⑭ on page 50
Actual-size pattern for ⑮ on page 48
Actual-size pattern for ⑯ on page 48

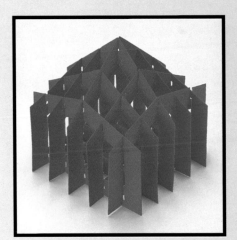

⑰

⑱

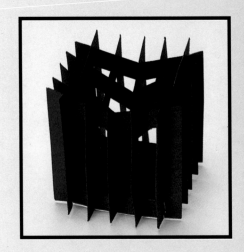

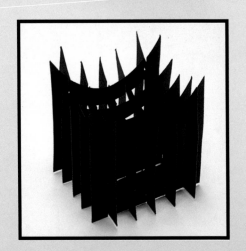

Actual-size pattern for ⑰ on page 47
Actual-size pattern for ⑱ on page 47

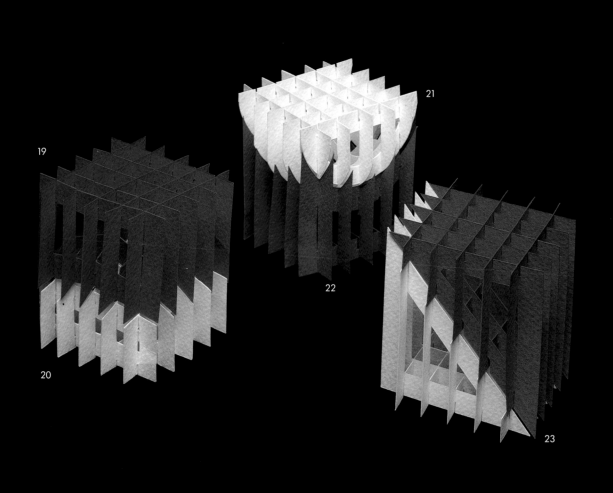

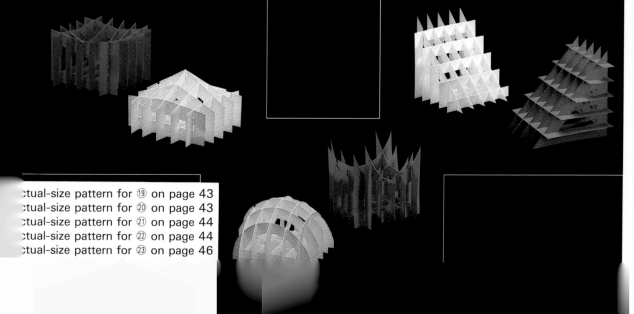

PAPER EGG

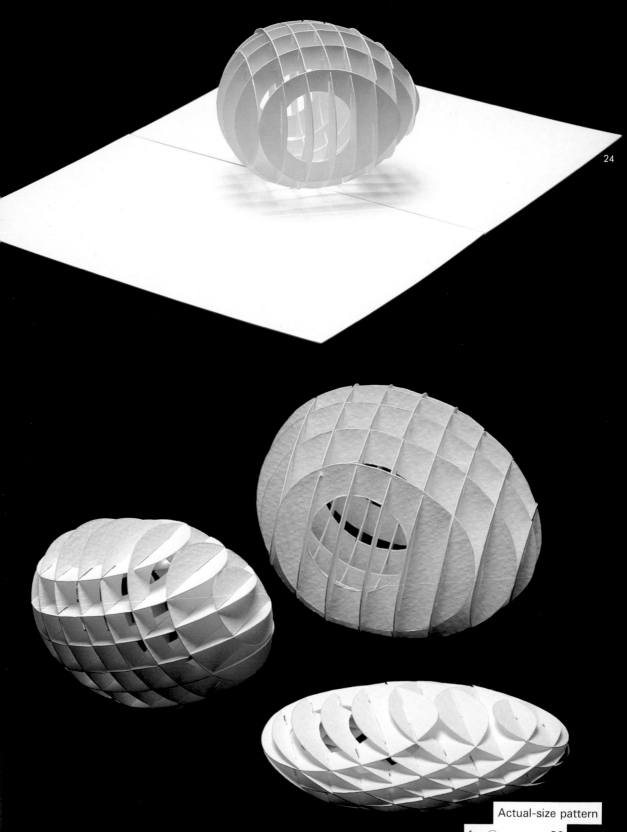

24

Actual-size pattern for ㉔ on page 60

13

THREE TREES

Actual-size pattern for ㉕ on page 55

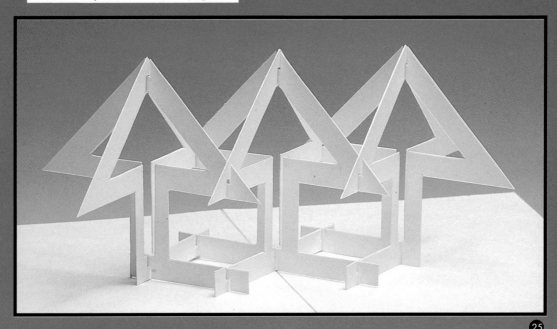

㉕

STADIUM

Actual-size pattern for ㉖ on page 83

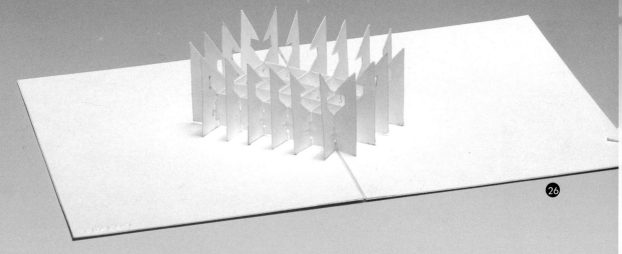

㉖

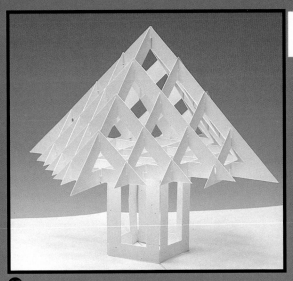

SNOW HOUSE
Actual-size pattern for ㉗ on page 84

㉗

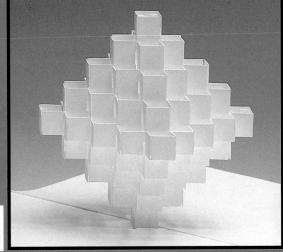

㉘

GROWING CRYSTAL
Actual-size pattern for ㉘ on page 81

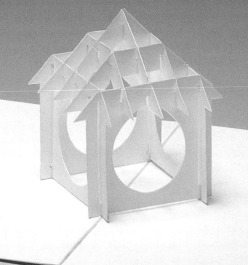

㉙

SUZHOU PRINCE REGENT'S PALACE
Actual-size pattern for ㉙ on page 80

MYSTERY BOX

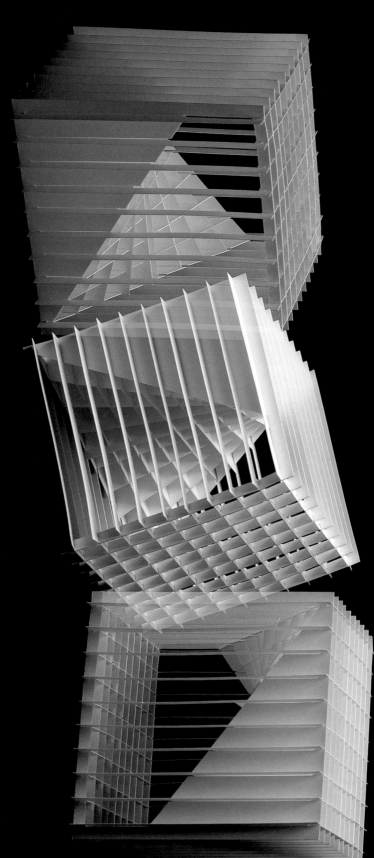

Actual-size pattern
for ㉚ on page 67

30

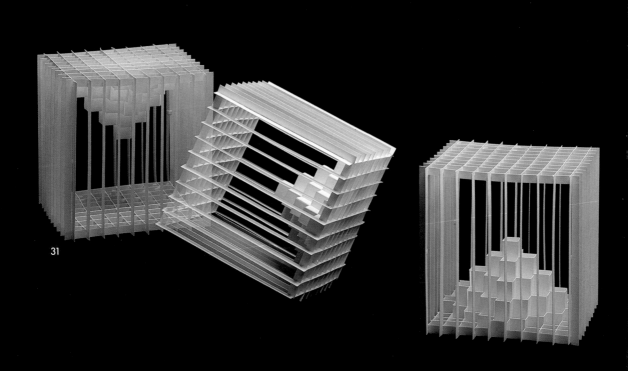

31

Actual-size pattern for ㉛ on page 72

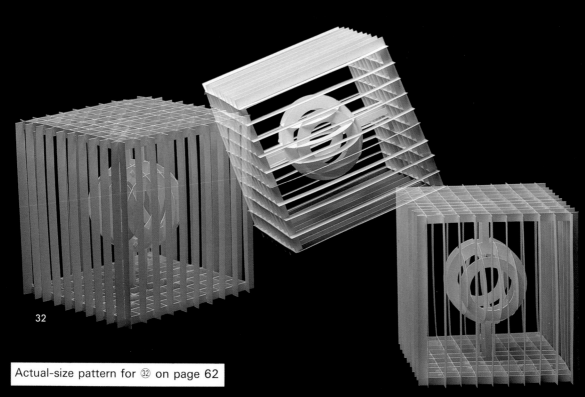

32

Actual-size pattern for ㉜ on page 62

LOOP

Actual-size pattern for ㉝ on page 77

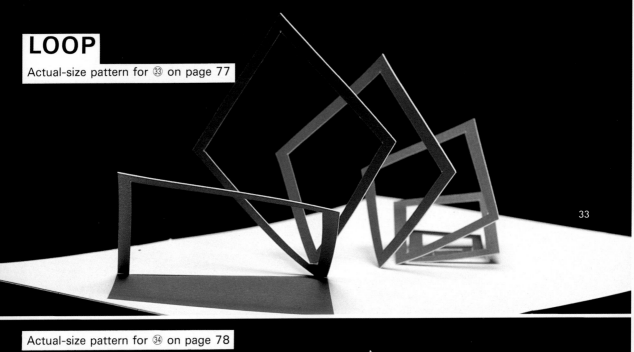

33

Actual-size pattern for ㉞ on page 78

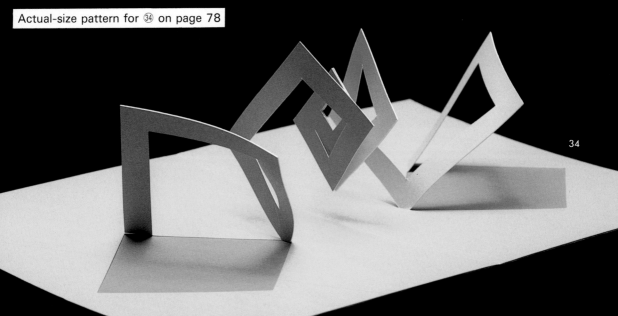

34

Actual-size pattern for ㉟ on page 32

35

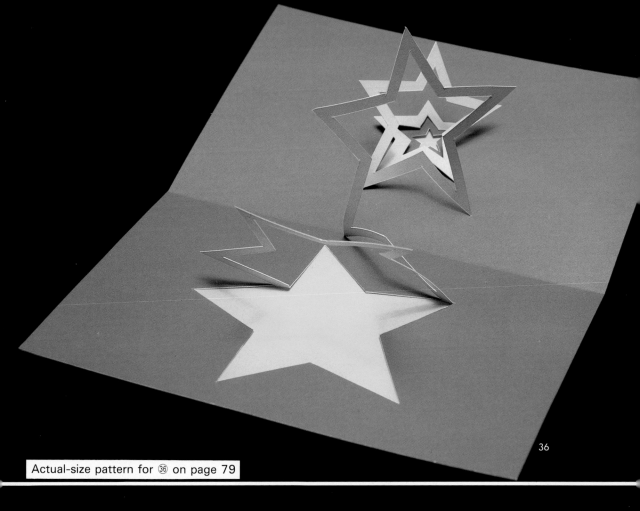

Actual-size pattern for ㊱ on page 79

36

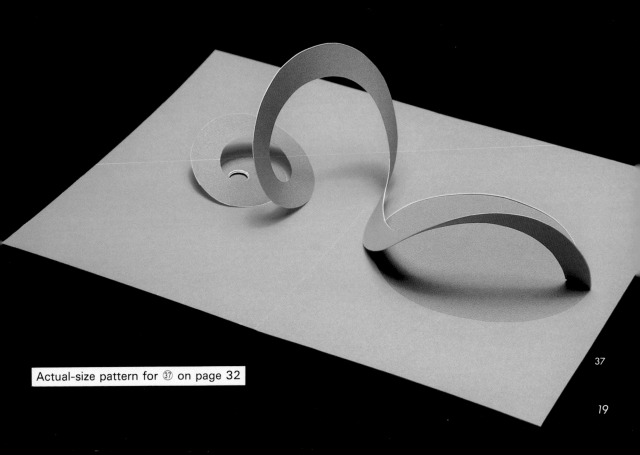

Actual-size pattern for ㊲ on page 32

37

CRYSTAL CARD

Actual-size pattern for ㉟ on page 65
Actual-size pattern for ㊴ on page 82
Actual-size pattern for ㊵ on page 29

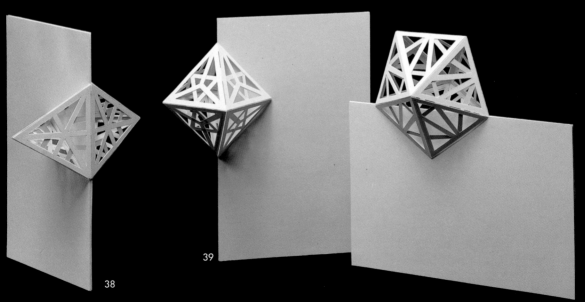

38

39

40

BASICS IN ORIGAMIC ARCHITECTURE

Materials and Tools

All the designs shown in this book can be made with simple materials and tools, but your hands and your head are the most important tools. Do your best to improve the crafts by using not only white paper, as in the previous designs, but also colored papers. You should personalize the crafts by using your favorite colors, not just those used in the examples. This time we will introduce many crafts that do not use a base paper in order that they may be used as interior designs, but all of them may be used as cards, as before, by putting them on the base paper with cotton thread.

Basic Materials and Tools

1. Bristol paper (to make practice patterns, use graph paper)
2. Two-colored construction paper (contrasting colors, front and back)
3. White duna paper, Colored duna paper
4. Sketch pad
5. Graph paper (1mm squares)
6. Pencil (HB or B)
7. Eraser
8. Tracing paper
9. Clear plastic ruler
10. Steel ruler
11. Protractor
12. Cutting knife (a circle cutter works well for curves)
13. Thick and thin styluses
14. Clear adhesive tape
15. Drafting tape
16. Compasses
17. Tweezers
18. All-purpose glue
19. White cotton thread
20. Japanese rice paper

About Papers

The origamic architecture in this book is different from previous designs in using many types of colored papers (colored construction paper, colored duna paper). Try to make each craft more interesting by using many different colored papers. Be extra careful while cutting out the small pieces to keep the craft strong.

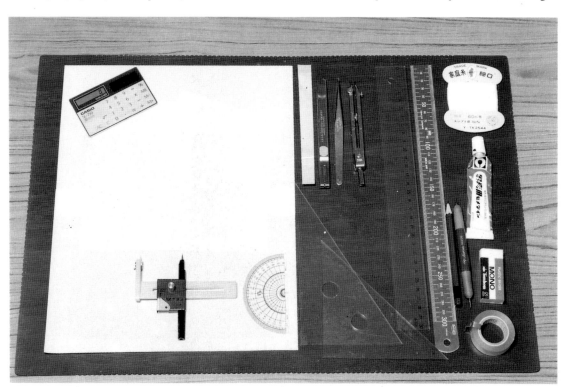

PRACTICE IN MAKING ORIGAMIC ARCHITECTURE

1) Pointers for Making Origamic Architecture

① How to cut the pattern

Place the traced pattern on a sheet of Bristol paper and transfer the pattern by perforating with a stylus. Using the cutting knife and steel ruler, cut along the perforated lines. When cutting sharp angles, cut each side toward the point. For curves, use circle cutter or draw curves with a pencil and cut along pencil lines freehand. Curves are best cut by moving both the paper and the cutter. These crafts involve much more joining of pieces than in previous editions, so it is important that the pattern be followed closely at irregular points and in making the lengths and widths of grooves. If the depth of the groove is wrong, the sides will not fit together correctly. Another key point is to begin cutting pieces by cutting the narrowest grooves. After cutting all the grooves, cut the outline. Make sure the cutting is done exactly along the lines.

HOW TO CUT SHARP ANGLES

② How to crease

A stylus is usually used for creasing. For a valley fold line score on the front side and for a mountain fold line score on the back. To make neat fold lines, cut to a depth of one-third of the paper on the front side. To make creation of your design easier and the final product more beautiful and work well, cut one-third way through the paper before making mountain or valley folds. Another way to do this is to put only the lightest pressure on the cutter and trace the pattern. In this way, mountain folds are cut on the front side and valley folds are cut on the back side.

③ How to glue the paper

Use all-purpose glue for assembling. It is not necessary to cover the entire surface. Be careful when putting glue near edges.

④ How to fold in half

In crafts which have a base, both papers must be folded so no edges protrude. If care is taken when crafts are being made, the edges should not protrude. If edges do protrude, place a steel ruler along the protruding edges and cut them off.

PROPER HANDLING OF PAPER

Fold lines should be put at right angles to grain of the paper. Both Bristol paper and duna paper are used in making origamic architecture in this book. The finished designs will look neat when they are handled properly. In the paper-making process, wood fibers tend to line up lengthwise, so most papers have a grain. When the wood fibers are aligned parallel to the long side of the paper it is called lengthwise-grain paper, and when the fibers are aligned parallel to the short side of the paper it is called crosswise-grain paper. When making 90-degree open-type designs, use lengthwise-grain paper. Paper is strongest when folded against the grain; when paper is folded with the grain it tends to bend and curl. To determine the grain of your paper, bend a 10cm (4") square. If the paper is easily folded, it has a lengthwise grain, if not, it has a crosswise grain.

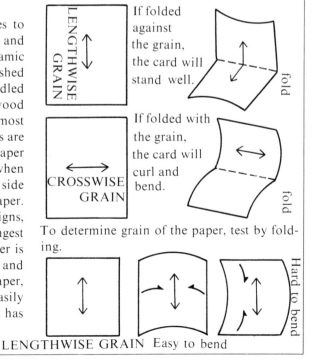

LENGTHWISE GRAIN

If folded against the grain, the card will stand well.

CROSSWISE GRAIN

If folded with the grain, the card will curl and bend.

To determine grain of the paper, test by folding.

LENGTHWISE GRAIN Easy to bend

Hard to bend

(2) How to Make Original Designs (Application)

① Sketch

Decide which pop-up design you can make by studying landscape photos and art in books and magazines. If you think you can make the design, make a sketch of it and develop a characteristic motif.

② Making your pattern

Transfer your sketch to graph paper. To ensure that the finished pattern fits on the paper, be sure to make a fold line across the middle of the sheet and check that the pattern does not extend past the edges of the sheet.

③ Prototype

After finishing the pattern, make the design using any craft paper at hand.

④ Improvement

As you make your prototype, you will discover the best places for cutting and folding, as well as places these should be avoided. Note these on the pattern. Any repairs can be made on the prototype using Scotch tape.

⑤ Full-size pattern

After noting the improvements, draw the full-size pattern, keeping in mind as you work the order of cutting and folding.

⑥ Completing the design

Trace the final pattern onto tracing paper. Place a sheet of Bristol paper beneath the tracing paper and perforate at the corners with a stylus. Connect the perforated points following the lines of the pattern. Proceed with cutting and folding of the lines. Follow the instructions of this book in making mountain and valley folds and you will have made your very own origamic architecture!

⑦ Adding accents

Study the whole design to see where you can best use colored papers for effective accents.

STEP-BY-STEP INSTRUCTIONS FOR MAKING DESIGNS ①
Designs ② and ③ COMBINED SHAPES
(shown on page 6)

① Materials
4 Sheets White duna paper 15cm x 12cm (6"x 5")
(2 sheets for the base)
2 Sheets colored duna paper 15cm x 12cm
(6"x 5")   Japanese rice paper and thread

② Copy the parts from the pattern by tracing or photocopying. Attach the copy onto a sheet of Bristol paper with drafting tape. Using a stylus, score the paper following the straight lines. Follow by copying the curved lines with the stylus.

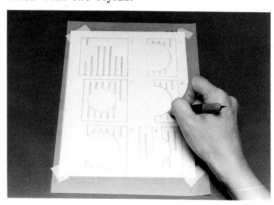

③ Remove the pattern and, using a steel ruler as a guide, cut the parts precisely.

23

④ After cutting all the parts, check again to make sure there are no errors, especially at irregular places.

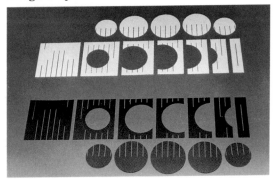

⑤ Refer to the assembly chart and assemble (A,a-G,g) ⑥ ⑦ ⑧

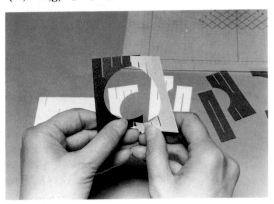

⑥

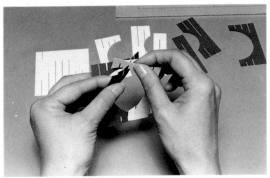

⑦

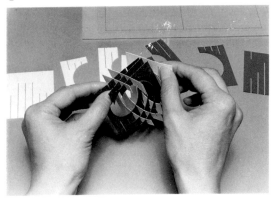

⑧ Run the thread through the four spots indicated and glue in place using tweezers to make a strong bond. Put glue on a small piece of Japanese rice paper (5mm x 5mm) and fix to one corner with this.

⑨ Make the base. Use the four 15cm x 20cm sheets of paper for the base and backing. Attach two sheets each together with rice paper, leaving a 1mm space for folding.

⑩ Place traced pattern of the base over the base and make marks at thread positions. Perforate base with a stylus.

⑪ Using tweezers, run the thread from the assembled design through the holes in the base.

⑫ Lightly attach thread to back of base with drafting tape.

⑬ Test tautness of thread by opening and closing base and adjust properly.

⑭ When thread is just right, glue it in place using rice paper.

⑮ Cut off extra thread and take off tape. Attach duna paper to backing and attach backing to base.

⑯ Cut off extra Japanese rice paper around edges of base.

⑰ Assemble sphere working outwards from the center. (Refer to assembly chart.)

⑱ Finished design.

25

Pattern

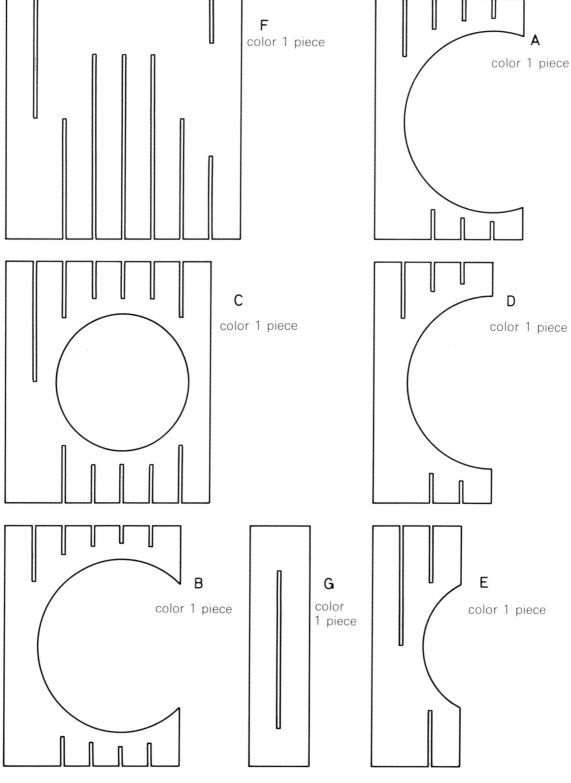

F
color 1 piece

A
color 1 piece

C
color 1 piece

D
color 1 piece

B
color 1 piece

G
color
1 piece

E
color 1 piece

Pattern

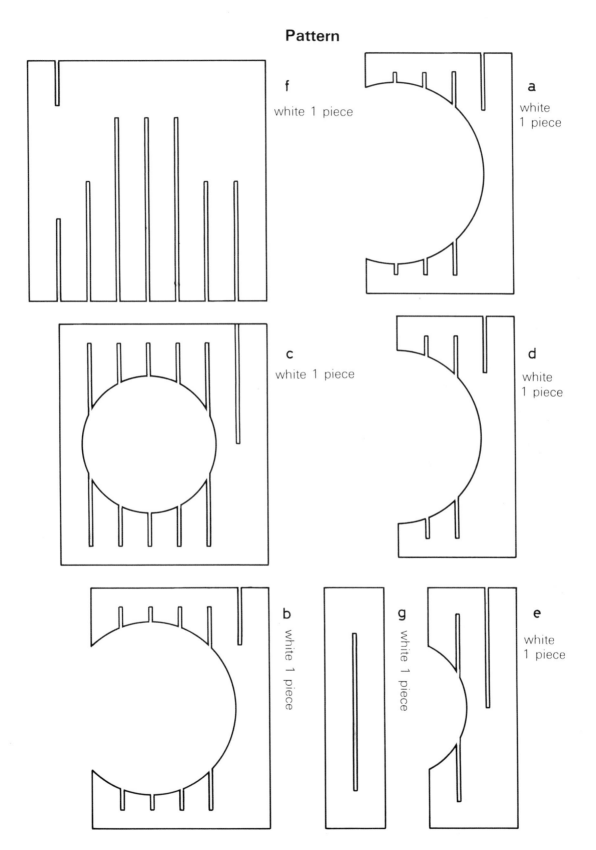

f
white 1 piece

a
white
1 piece

c
white 1 piece

d
white
1 piece

b white 1 piece

g white 1 piece

e
white
1 piece

Pattern

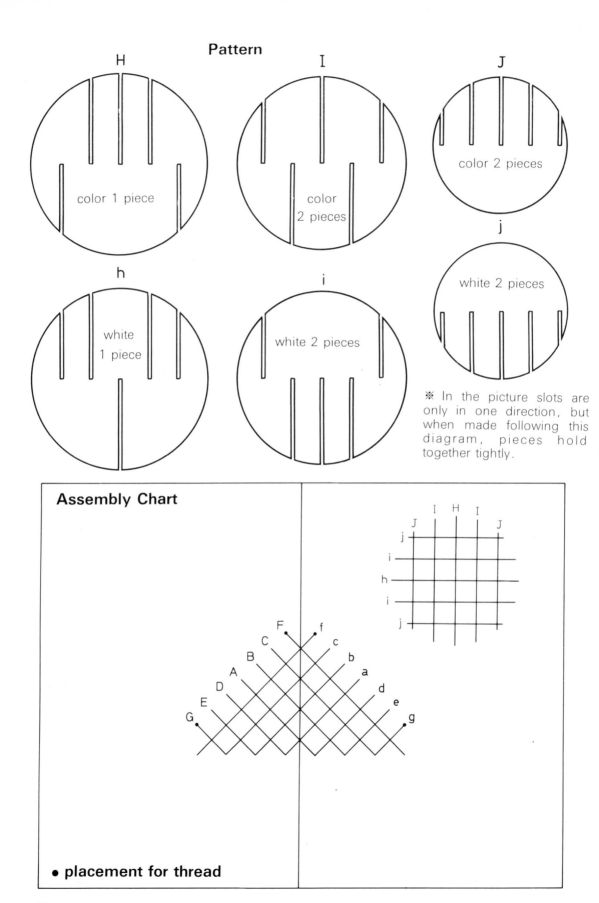

H color 1 piece

I color 2 pieces

J color 2 pieces

j white 2 pieces

h white 1 piece

i white 2 pieces

※ In the picture slots are only in one direction, but when made following this diagram, pieces hold together tightly.

Assembly Chart

● **placement for thread**

STEP-BY-STEP INSTRUCTIONS FOR MAKING DESIGNS ②
Design 40 CRYSTAL CARD (Decahedron) (shown on page 20)

① Materials
3 Sheets White Bristol Paper 15cm × 20cm (6″ × 8″)
1 Sheet Colored Bristol paper 15cm × 20cm (6″ × 8″)

② Copy parts from the patterns by tracing or photocopying.

③ Attach the copy to a sheet of Bristol paper with drafting tape. Using a stylus perforate the paper at corners and intersections.

④ Remove the pattern and, using a steel ruler as a guide, cut the parts precisely. There are ten white pieces.

⑤ Cut the 10 colored pieces from colored Bristol paper as in ③ and ④.

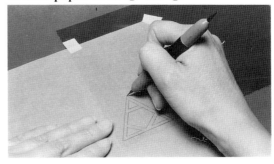

⑥ Make sure all parts are cut properly.

⑦ Refer to Assembly chart and arrange the 10 white parts as shown. Put glue on small pieces of Japanese rice paper and use these to glue sides at three places as shown.

⑧ Attach four threads at places as indicated and fasten in place with glue and rice paper.

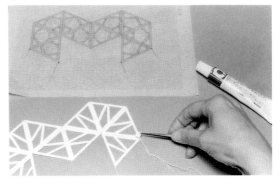

Pattern

white Bristol paper 10 pieces

colored Bristol paper 10 pieces

Point

For the hexahedron, octahedron, and decahedron, the white pieces are first attached together with small pieces of Japanese rice paper and glue (be careful not to cut the rice paper too large). When gluing the Canford paper, be careful to hide the Japanese rice paper and thread.

Placement Figure

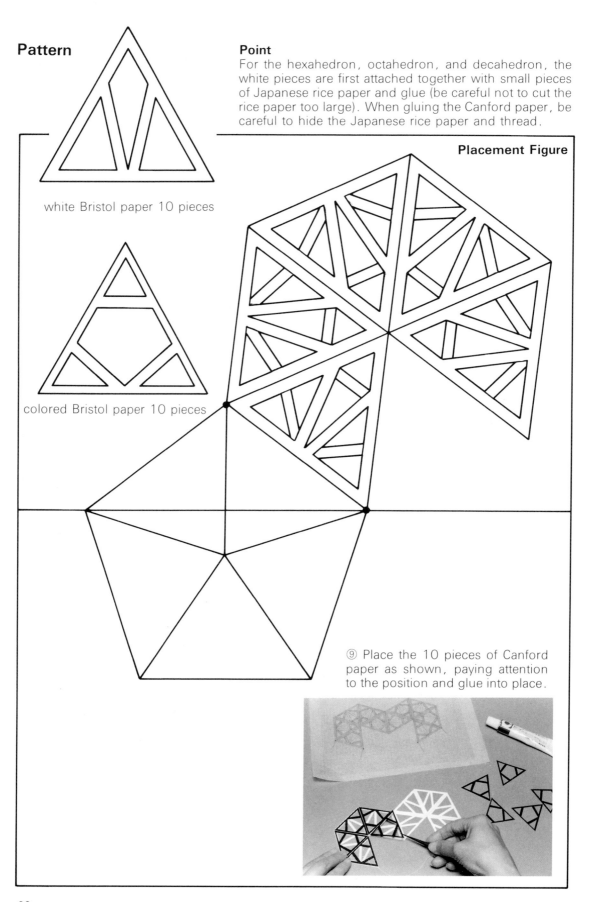

⑨ Place the 10 pieces of Canford paper as shown, paying attention to the position and glue into place.

⑩ Make sure the assembled form matches the pattern.

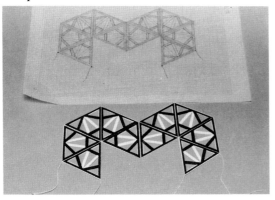

⑪ Refer to the gluing figure. Glue points A and a and B and b with Japanese rice paper.

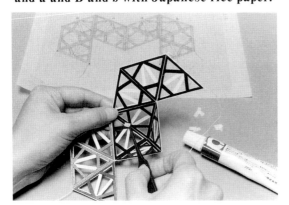

⑫ Make the base by attaching two 15cm × 20cm (6″ × 8″) sheets of Bristol paper together with glue and Japanese rice paper. Put the placement figure on the base. Align center line of the placement figure with center line of the base at the three points of symmetry and make holes with a stylus at the places at the points indicated.

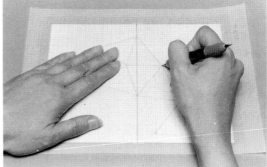

Gluing Figure

• thread placement

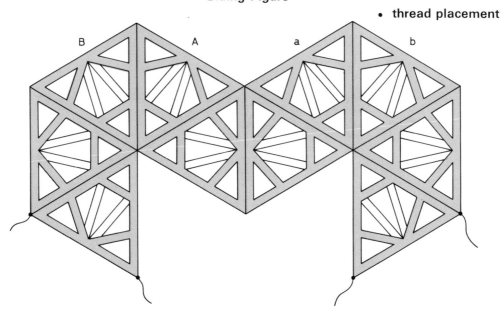

B   A   a   b

⑬ Using tweezers, insert each of the two middle threads of the assembled form through the hole at the center line of the base and each of the outside threads through the other hole.

⑭ Lightly fasten each of the four threads to the base with drafting tape.

⑮ Completely unfold the base and adjust the tension of the thread and check the alignment of the edges of the base.

⑯ After adjusting, fasten the thread in place with glue and Japanese rice paper.

⑰ Cut off excess thread and remove drafting tape. Make backing with two sheets of 15cm × 10cm (6″ × 4″) Bristol paper.

⑱ Cut off any protruding Japanese rice paper around edges.

⑲ Finished design.

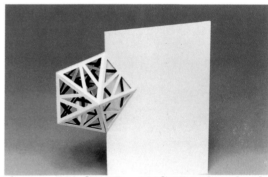

STEP-BY-STEP INSTRUCTIONS FOR MAKING DESIGNS ③
Designs ㉟ and ㊲ LOOP
(shown on pages 18-19)
① Materials
2 Sheets Bristol paper 15cm × 20cm (6″ × 8″)
※ This design is most interesting when made with two-color construction paper (contrasting colors front and back).

② Copy the pattern onto tracing paper or photocopy.

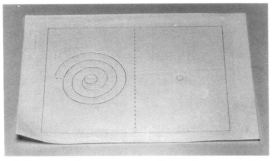

③ Fasten the copy onto Bristol paper with drafting tape. Using a stylus, perforate along the lines and scribe the curved lines from the pattern to the Bristol paper with a stylus.

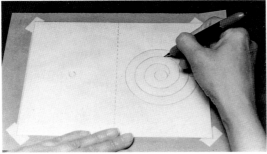

④ Remove the pattern and, using a steel ruler, cut the straight line precisely with a stylus. Cut the curved lines freehand by moving the paper a bit as you cut.

⑤ Put a steel ruler along the fold lines and use a cutting knife to cut halfway through the paper. Cut the mountain folds on the front and the valley folds on the back.

⑥ Lift out the cut portion.

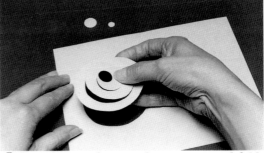

⑦ Put glue on the attachment spot and fold paper in half.

⑧ Use two 10cm × 15cm (4″ × 6″) sheets of Bristol paper as backing. Glue the paper to the design so the front of the base is the same color as the back of the design.

33

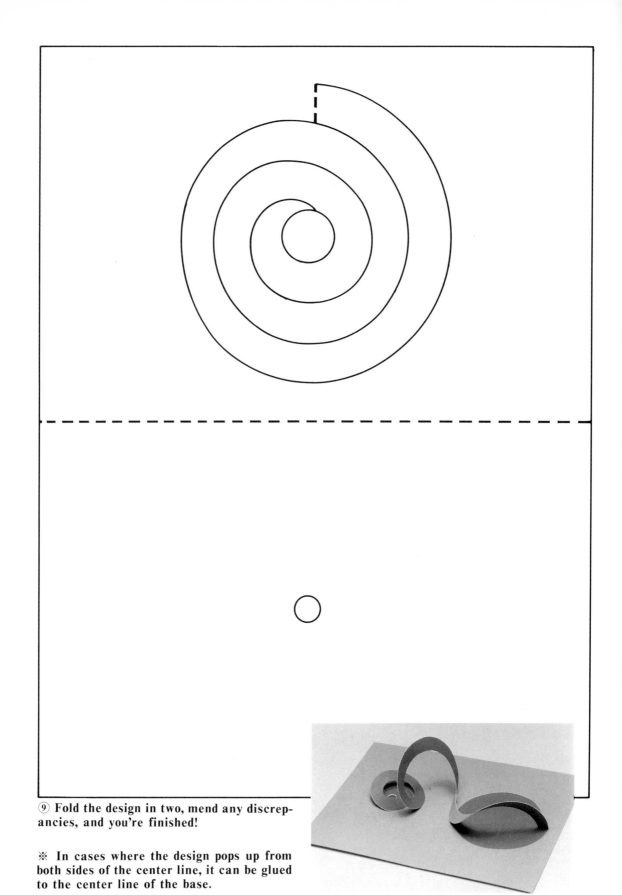

⑨ Fold the design in two, mend any discrepancies, and you're finished!

※ In cases where the design pops up from both sides of the center line, it can be glued to the center line of the base.

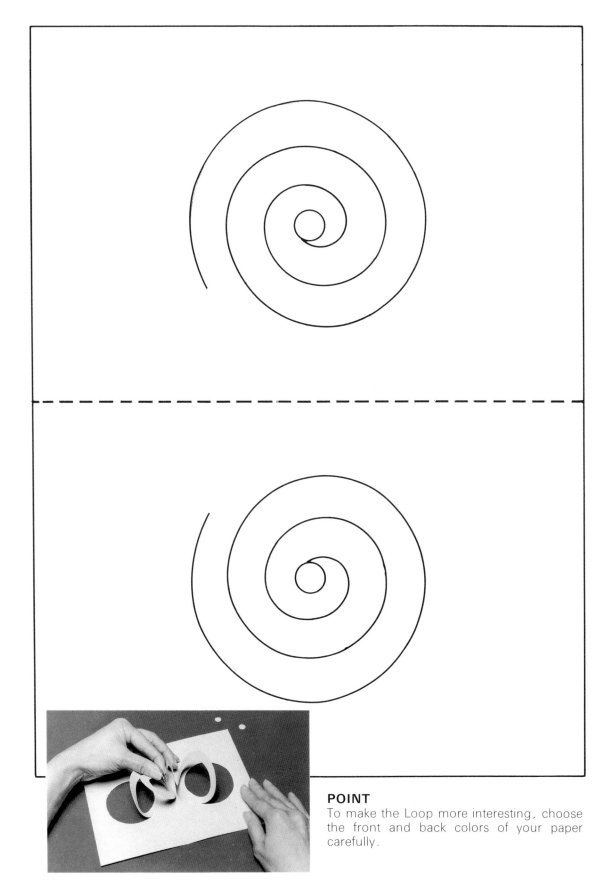

POINT
To make the Loop more interesting, choose the front and back colors of your paper carefully.

ACTUAL SIZE DIAGRAMS
AND INSTRUCTIONS

Completion Figure

Assembly Figure

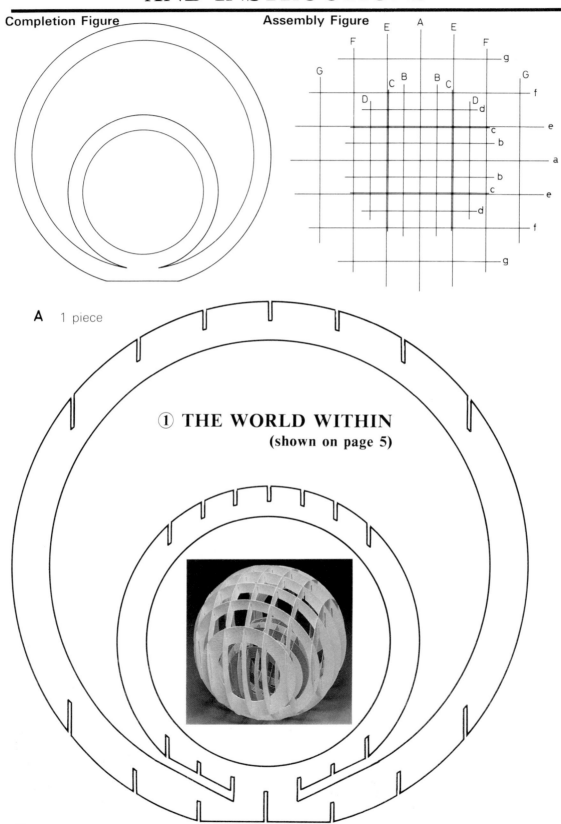

A 1 piece

① **THE WORLD WITHIN**
(shown on page 5)

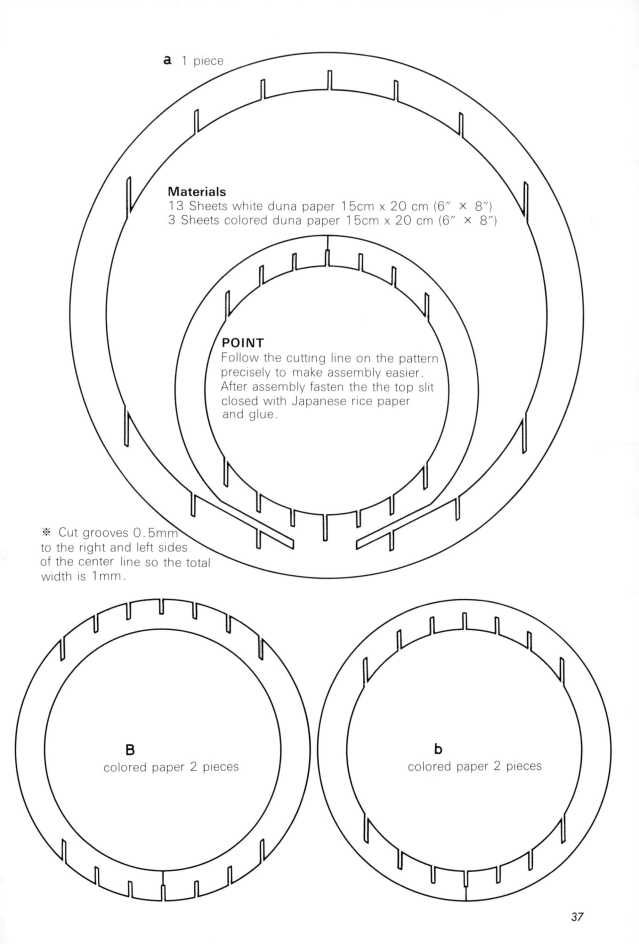

a 1 piece

Materials
13 Sheets white duna paper 15cm x 20 cm (6″ × 8″)
3 Sheets colored duna paper 15cm x 20 cm (6″ × 8″)

POINT
Follow the cutting line on the pattern
precisely to make assembly easier.
After assembly fasten the the top slit
closed with Japanese rice paper
and glue.

※ Cut grooves 0.5mm
to the right and left sides
of the center line so the total
width is 1mm.

B
colored paper 2 pieces

b
colored paper 2 pieces

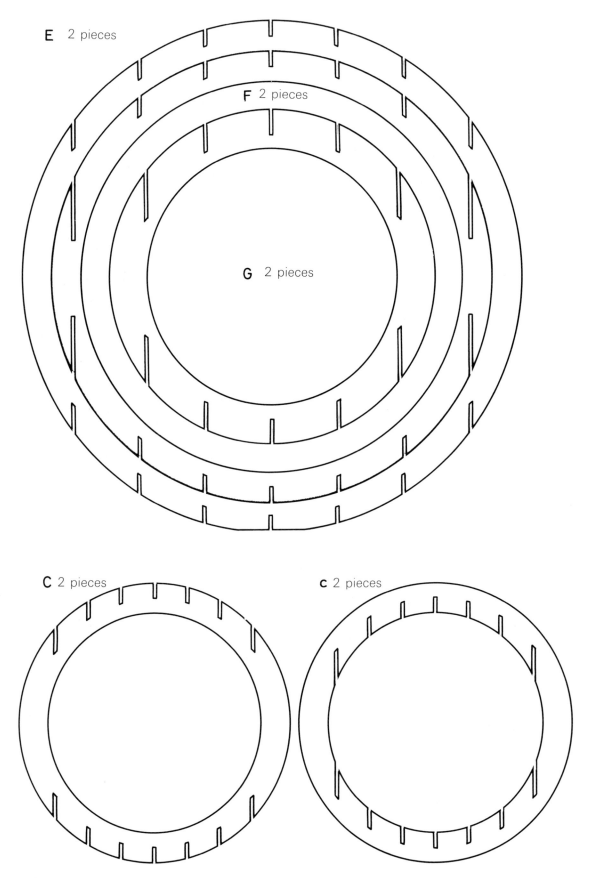

E 2 pieces

F 2 pieces

G 2 pieces

C 2 pieces

c 2 pieces

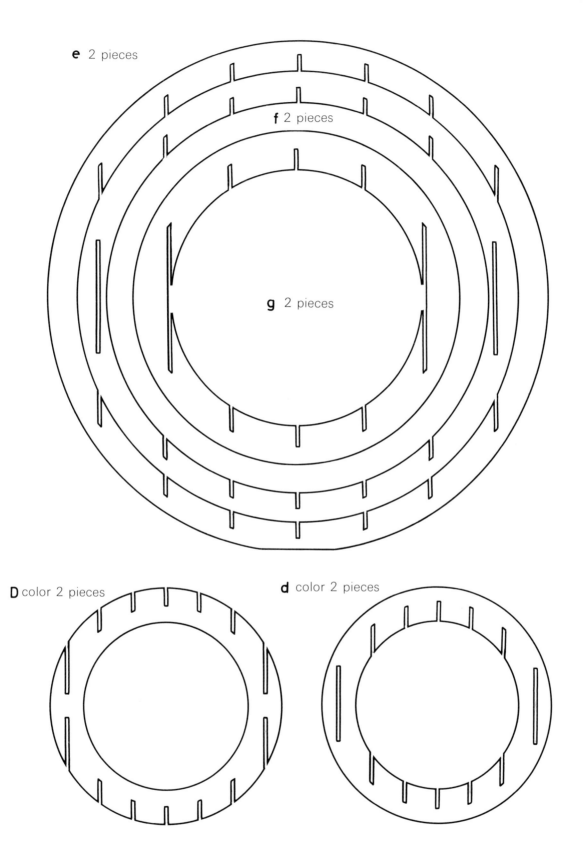

e 2 pieces

f 2 pieces

g 2 pieces

D color 2 pieces

d color 2 pieces

⑩ TETRAHEDRON (shown on page 8)

Materials
2 Sheets colored duna paper
15cm x 20cm (6″ × 8″)

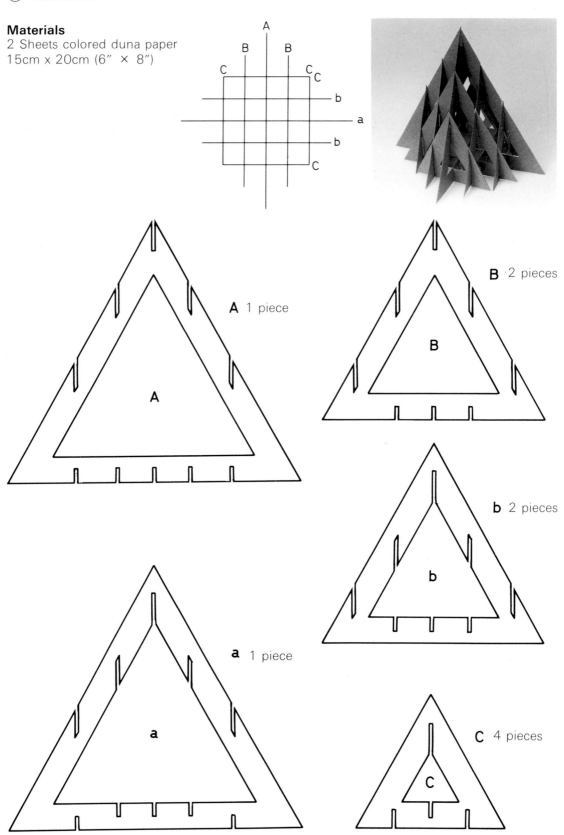

A 1 piece

B 2 pieces

b 2 pieces

a 1 piece

C 4 pieces

⑫ DIAMOND (shown on page 9)

Materials
2 Sheets colored duna paper
15cm x 20cm (6″ × 8″)

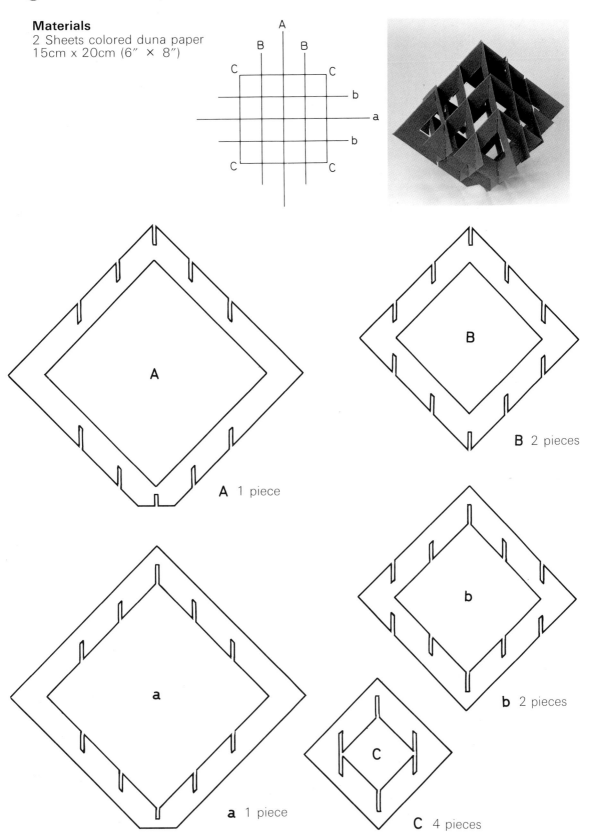

A 1 piece

B 2 pieces

a 1 piece

b 2 pieces

C 4 pieces

⑬ HEMISPHERE
(shown on page 9)

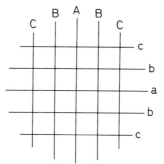

Materials
2 Sheets colored duna paper
15cm x 20cm (6″ × 8″)

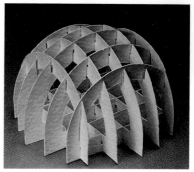

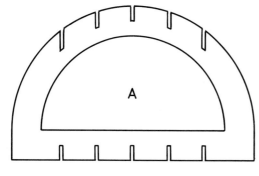

A

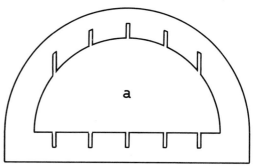

a

A、a 1 piece each

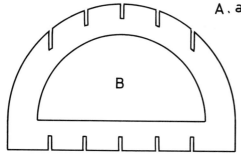

B

b

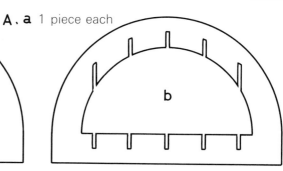

B・b
C・c } 2 pieces each

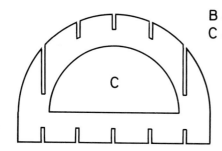

C

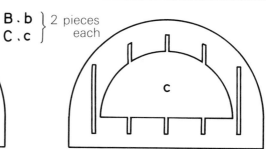

c

⑪ CUBIC COMBINATIONS
(shown on page 8)

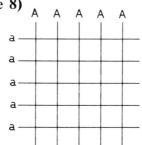

Materials
2 Sheets colored duna paper
15cm x 20cm (6″ × 8″)

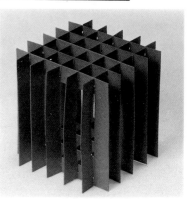

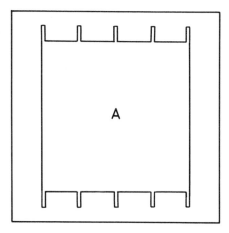

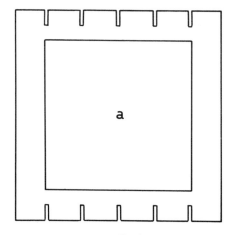

A 5 pieces

a 5 pieces

⑲, ⑳ CUBIC COMBINATIONS

(shown on page 12)

Materials
1 Sheet white duna paper
15cm x 20cm (6″ × 8″)
1 Sheet colored duna paper
15cm x 20cm (6″ × 8″)

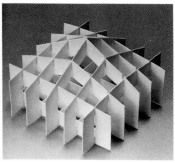

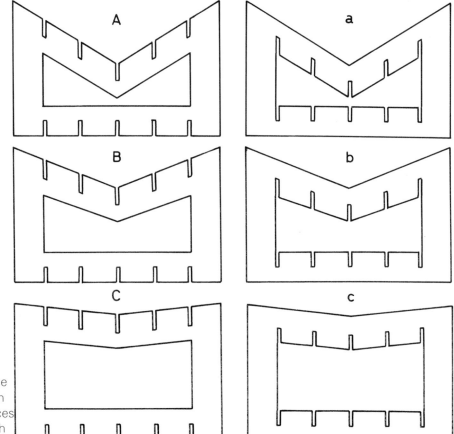

A · a 1 piece each
B · b 2 pieces each
C · c

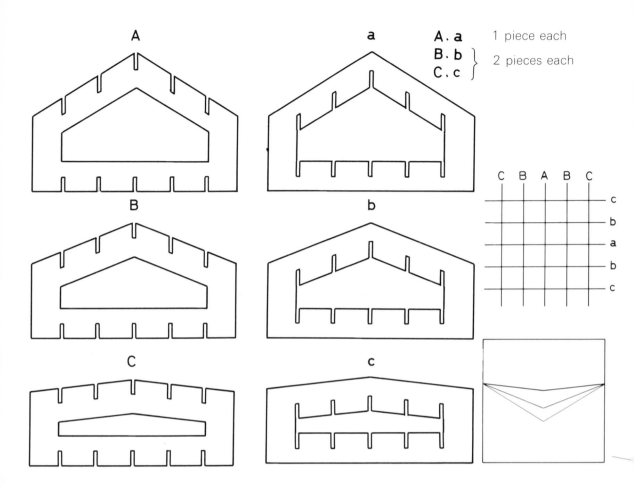

A   a   A . a   1 piece each

B   b   B . b

C   c   C . c   2 pieces each

㉑, ㉒ INTERLOCKING HEMISPHERE AND CUBE

(shown on page 12)

Materials
2 Sheets white duna paper
15cm x 20cm (6″ × 8″)
2 Sheets colored duna paper
15cm x 20 cm (6″ × 8″)

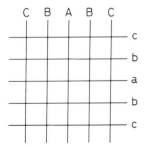
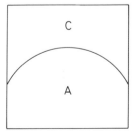
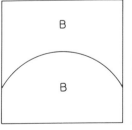
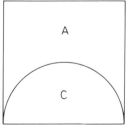

44

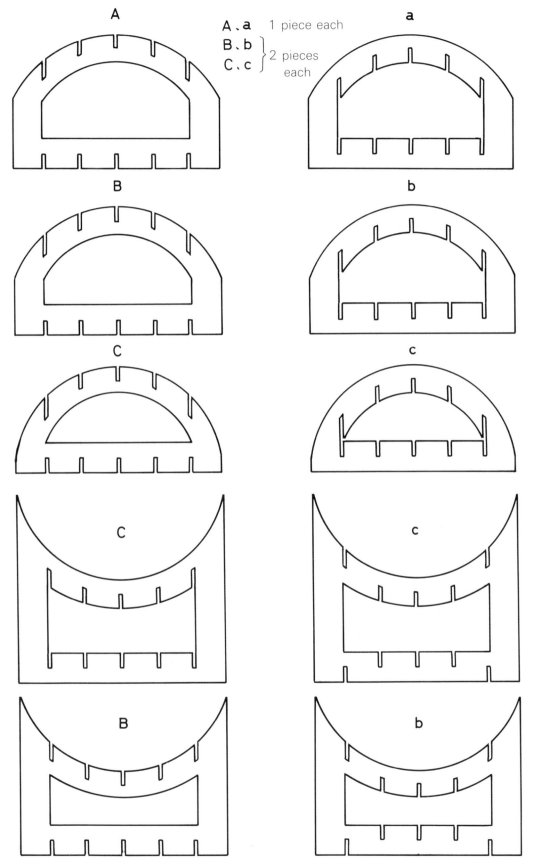

A

A、a 1 piece each
B、b } 2 pieces
C、c } each

a

B

b

C

c

C

c

B

b

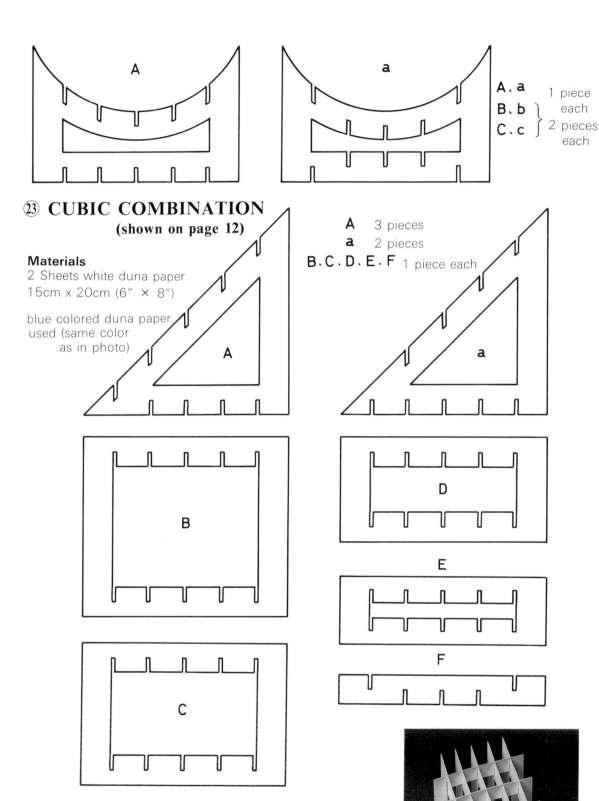

㉓ CUBIC COMBINATION
(shown on page 12)

Materials
2 Sheets white duna paper
15cm x 20cm (6″ × 8″)

blue colored duna paper
used (same color
as in photo)

A·a   1 piece each
B·b
C·c } 2 pieces each

A   3 pieces
a   2 pieces
B·C·D·E·F 1 piece each

A

a

B

C

D

E

F

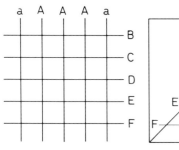

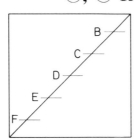

⑰, ⑱ RECTANGLE COMBINATIONS

(shown on page 11)

Materials

2 Sheets colored duna paper (red)
15cm x 20 cm (6″ × 8″)
2 Sheets colored duna paper (black)
15cm x 20cm (6″ × 8″)

A、a   1 piece each
B、b   } 2 pieces
C、c   each

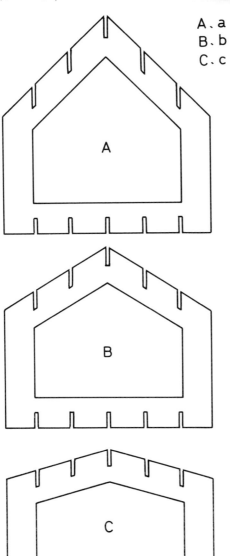

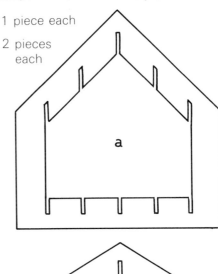

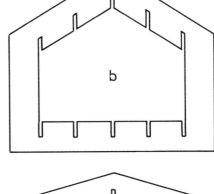

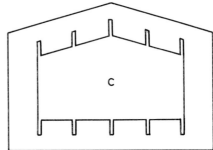

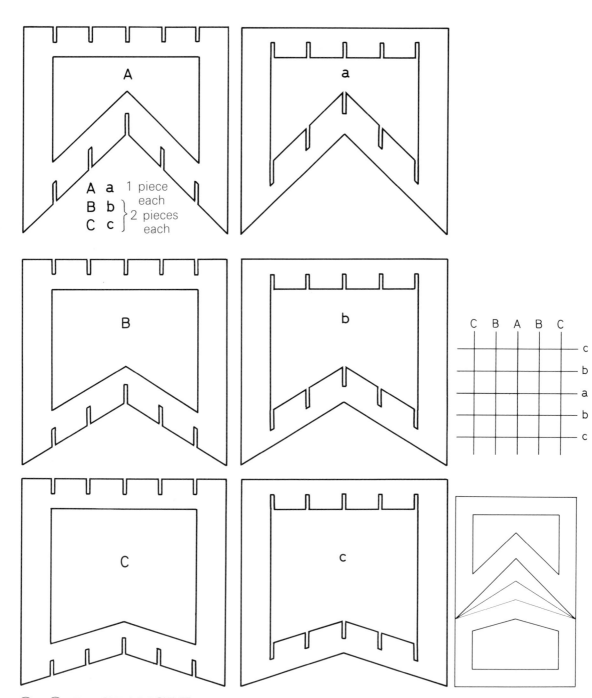

A   a   1 piece each
B   b
C   c   } 2 pieces each

⑮, ⑯ RECTANGLE COMBINATIONS
(shown on page 10)

Materials
2 Sheets colored duna paper (red)
15cm x 20cm (6″ × 8″)
2 Sheets colored duna paper (black)
15cm x 20cm (6″ × 8″)

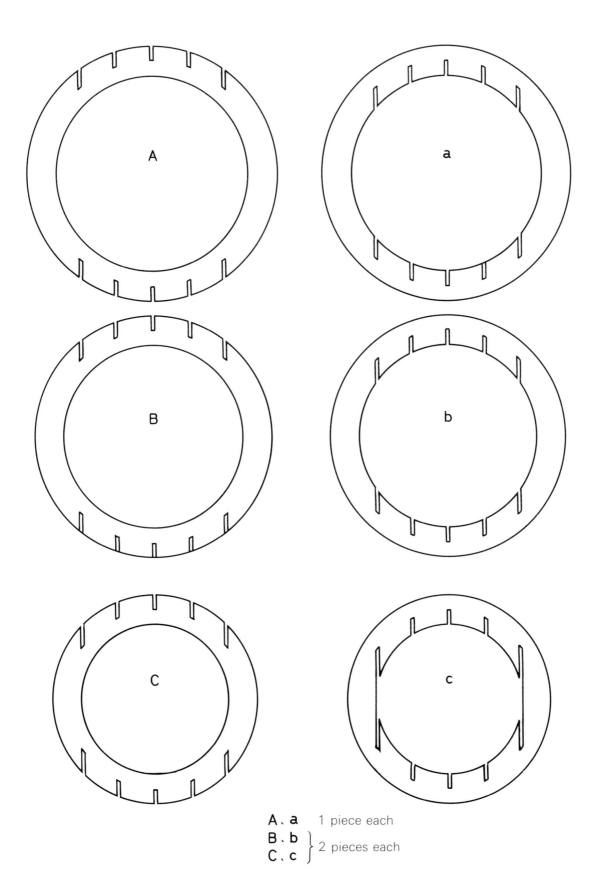

A、a   1 piece each
B、b
C、c } 2 pieces each

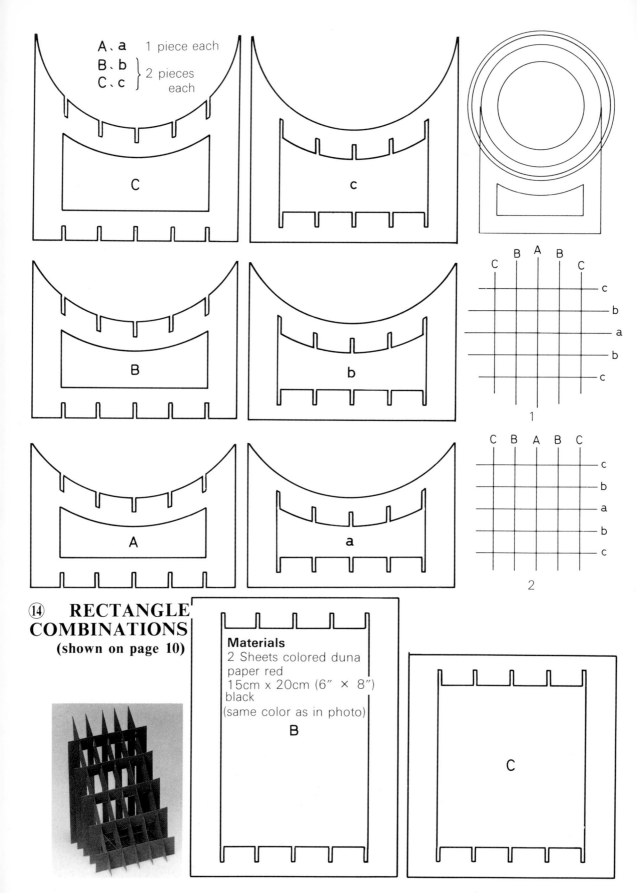

A、a 1 piece each
B、b } 2 pieces
C、c } each

C

c

B

b

A

a

C B A B C
c
b
a
b
c

1

C B A B C
c
b
a
b
c

2

⑭ **RECTANGLE COMBINATIONS**
(shown on page 10)

Materials
2 Sheets colored duna paper red
15cm x 20cm (6″ × 8″) black
(same color as in photo)

B

C

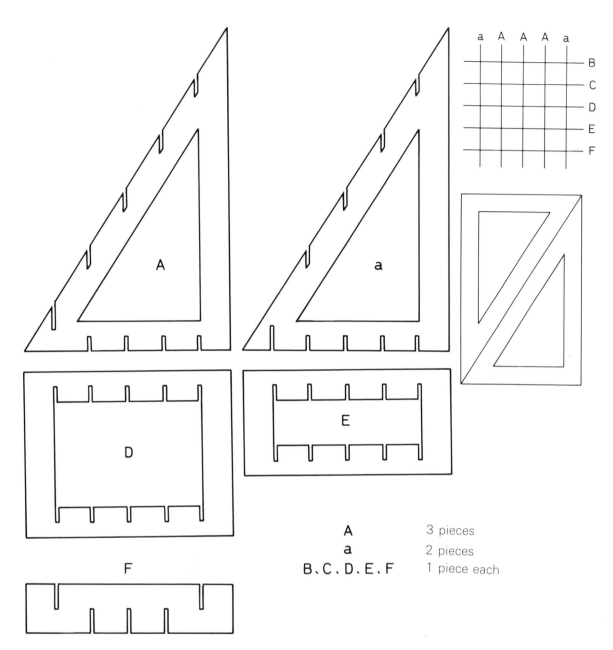

a A A A a
B
C
D
E
F

A

a

D

E

F

A   3 pieces
a   2 pieces
B、C、D、E、F   1 piece each

⑥, ⑦ COMBINATION SHAPES (shown on page 7)

Materials

5 Sheets white duna paper
15cm x 20cm (6" × 8")
   (3 sheets for parts,
    2 sheets for base)

1 Sheet colored duna paper
15cm x 20cm (6" × 8")
Japanese rice paper small piece

Thread small piece

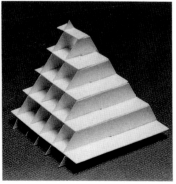

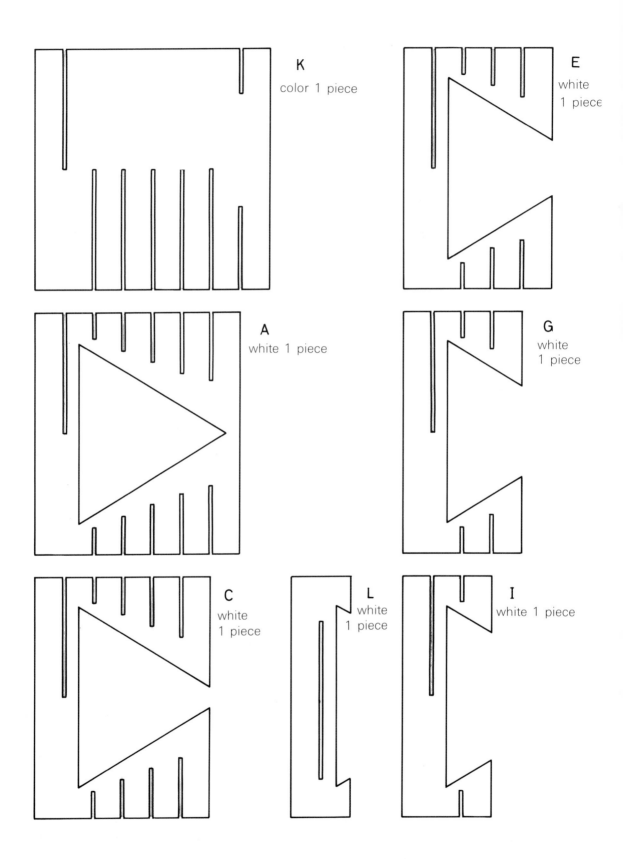

K
color 1 piece

E
white
1 piece

A
white 1 piece

G
white
1 piece

C
white
1 piece

L
white
1 piece

I
white 1 piece

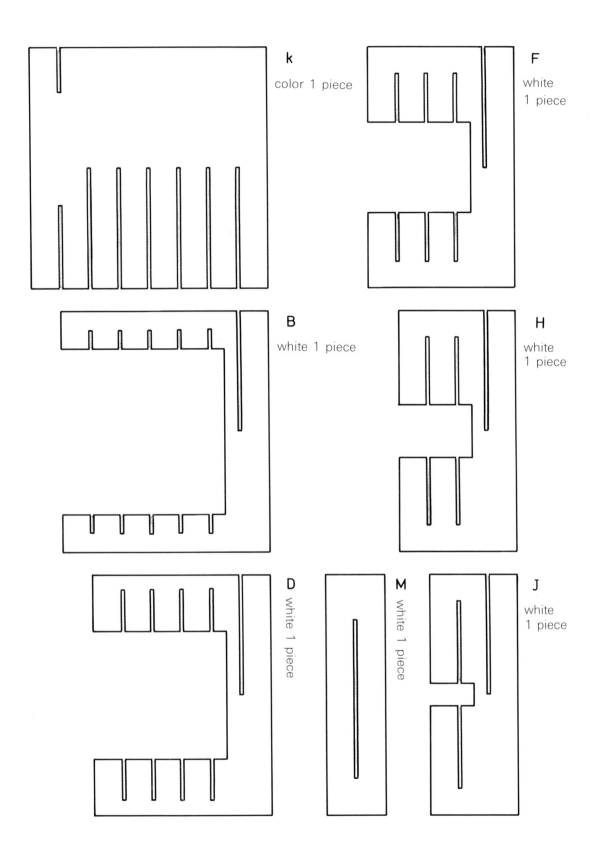

k

color 1 piece

F

white
1 piece

B

white 1 piece

H

white
1 piece

D white 1 piece

M white 1 piece

J

white
1 piece

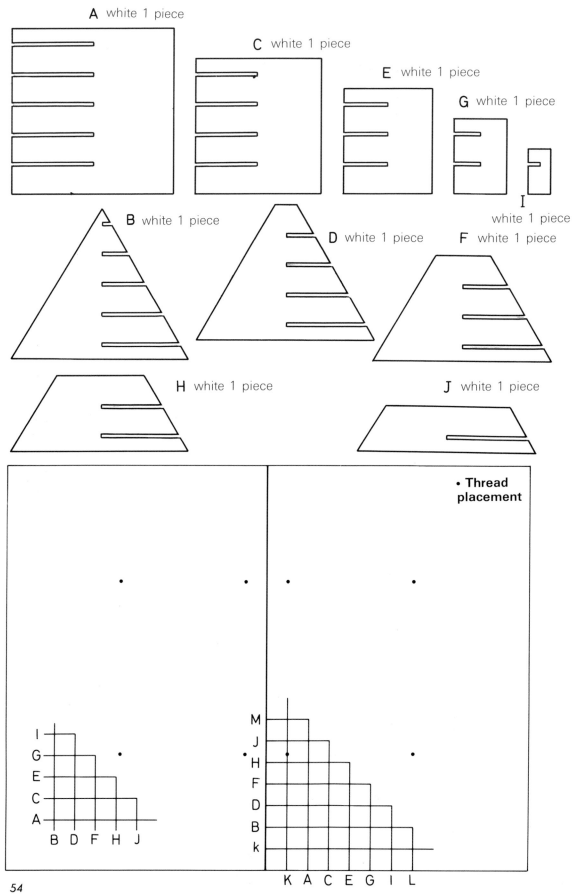

A white 1 piece
C white 1 piece
E white 1 piece
G white 1 piece
I white 1 piece
B white 1 piece
D white 1 piece
F white 1 piece
H white 1 piece
J white 1 piece

• Thread placement

54

㉕ THREE TREES
(shown on page 14)

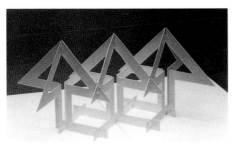

Materials
3 Sheets white Bristol paper
(1 sheet for parts, 2 sheets for base)
Japanese rice paper small piece
Thread small piece

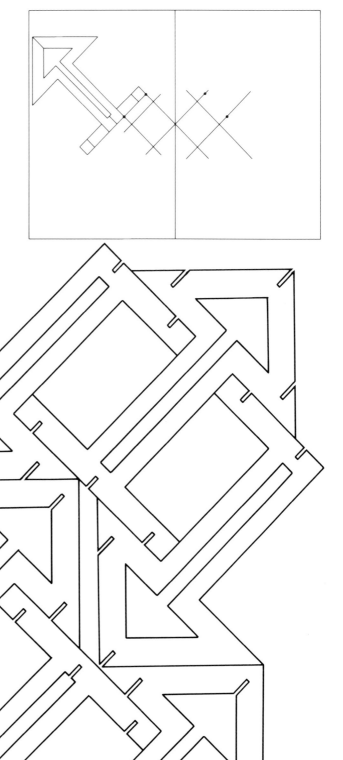

④, ⑤ COMBINATION SHAPES (shown on page 6)

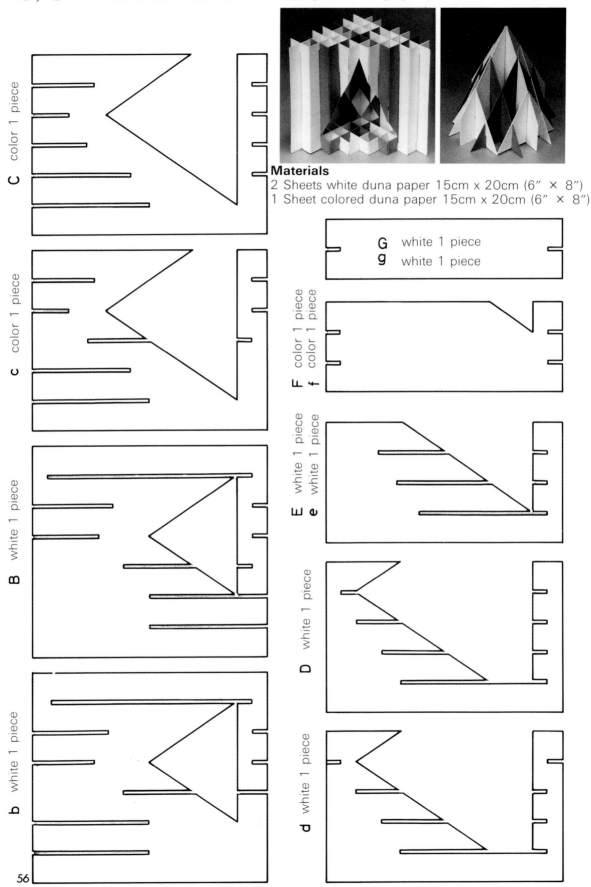

Materials
2 Sheets white duna paper 15cm x 20cm (6″ × 8″)
1 Sheet colored duna paper 15cm x 20cm (6″ × 8″)

C color 1 piece

c color 1 piece

B white 1 piece

b white 1 piece

G white 1 piece
g white 1 piece

F color 1 piece
f color 1 piece

E white 1 piece
e white 1 piece

D white 1 piece

d white 1 piece

A white 1 piece

a white 1 piece

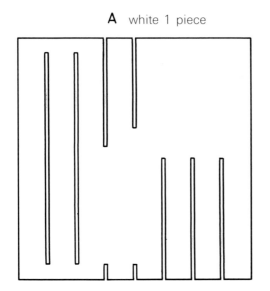
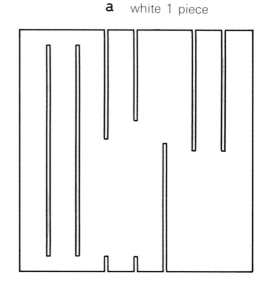

a white 1 piece

b color 1 piece
white 1 piece

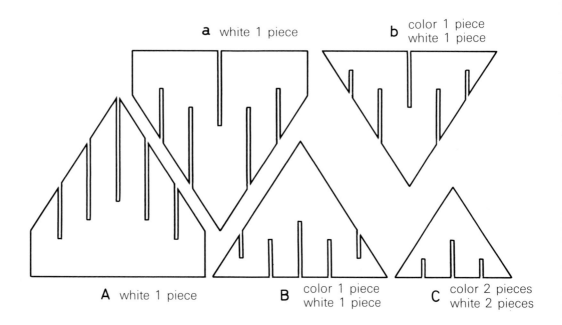

A white 1 piece

B color 1 piece
white 1 piece

C color 2 pieces
white 2 pieces

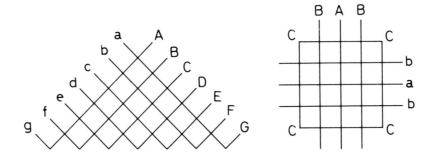

⑧, ⑨ COMBINATION SHAPES (shown on page 7)

Materials
2 Sheets white duna paper
15cm x 20cm (6″ × 8″)
2 Sheets colored duna paper
15cm x 20 cm (6″ × 8″)

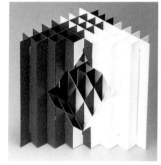

A color 1 piece

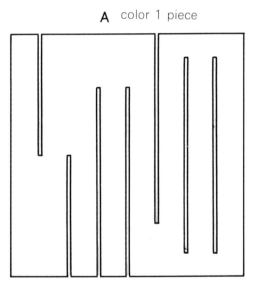

B color 1 piece

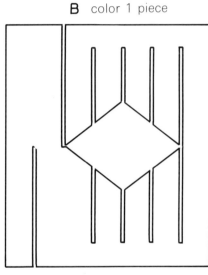

F white 1 piece
f color 1 piece

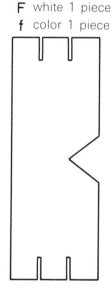

a white 1 piece

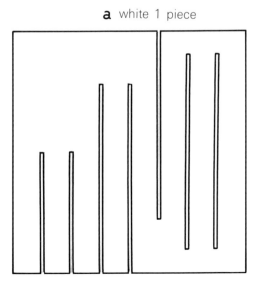

b white 1 piece

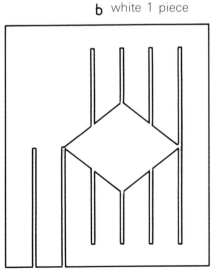

G white 1 piece
g color 1 piece

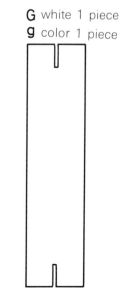

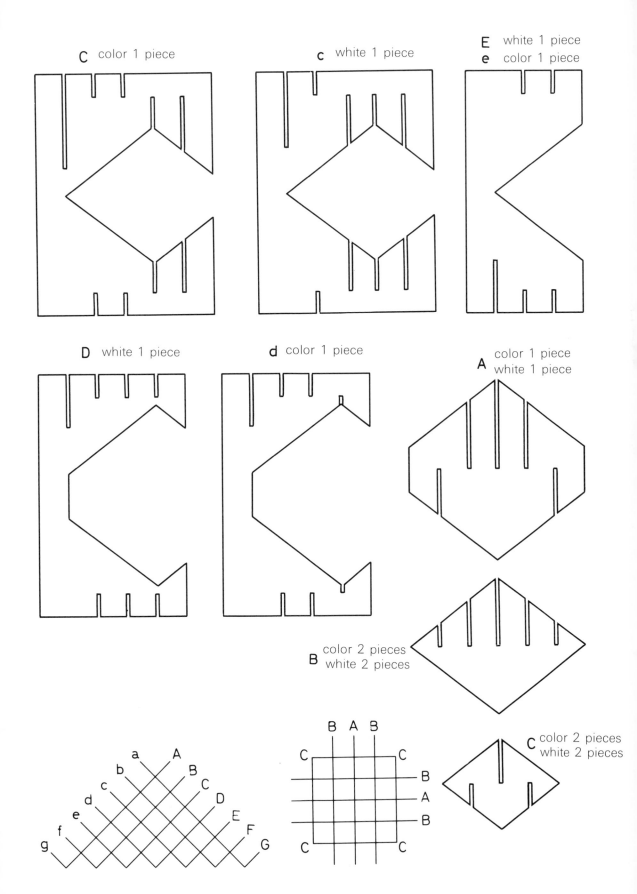

C color 1 piece

c white 1 piece

E white 1 piece
e color 1 piece

D white 1 piece

d color 1 piece

A color 1 piece
white 1 piece

B color 2 pieces
white 2 pieces

C color 2 pieces
white 2 pieces

㉔ PAPER EGG (shown on page 13)

Materials

4 Sheets white Bristol paper 15cm x 20cm (6″ × 8″)
(2 sheets for parts, 2 sheets for base)
Japanese rice paper small piece
Thread small piece

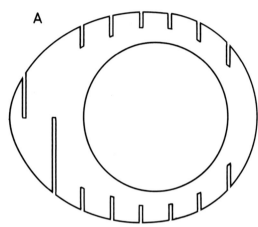

A

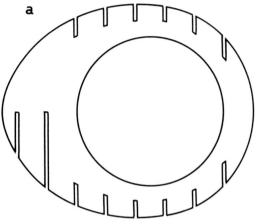

a

A.a.E.F.G.H.I.J 1 piece each

B.C.D 2 pieces each

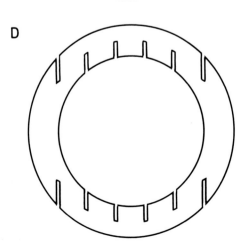

B

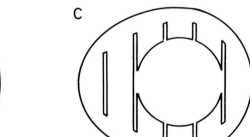

C

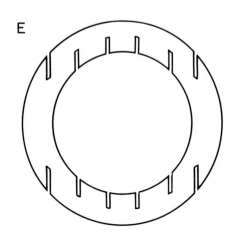

D

E

60

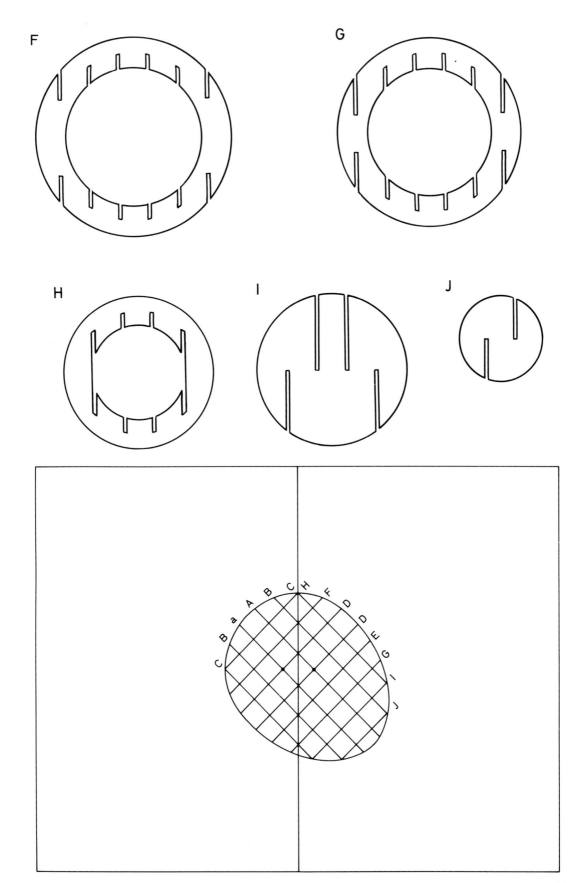

㉜ MYSTERY BOX (shown on page 17)

A
2 pieces

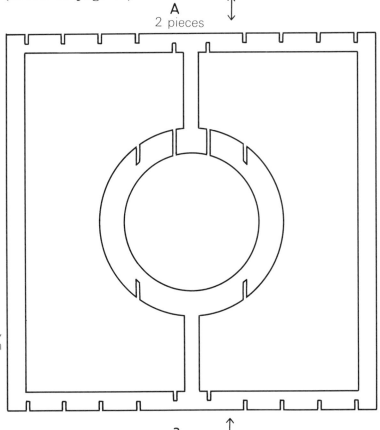

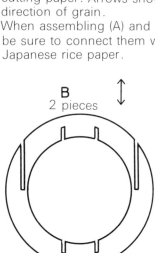

Materials
7 Sheets white Bristol paper
15cm x 20cm (6″ × 8″)

POINT
Be careful of grain when
cutting paper. Arrows show
direction of grain.
When assembling (A) and (a),
be sure to connect them with
Japanese rice paper.

B
2 pieces

a
2 pieces

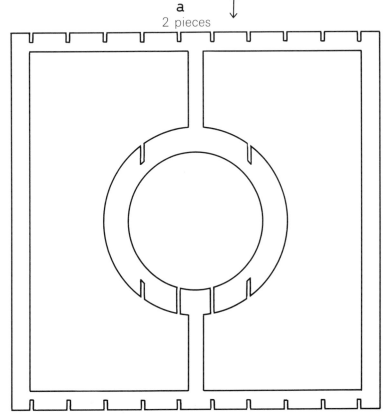

b
2 pieces

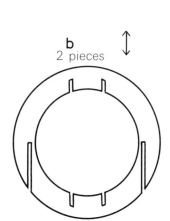

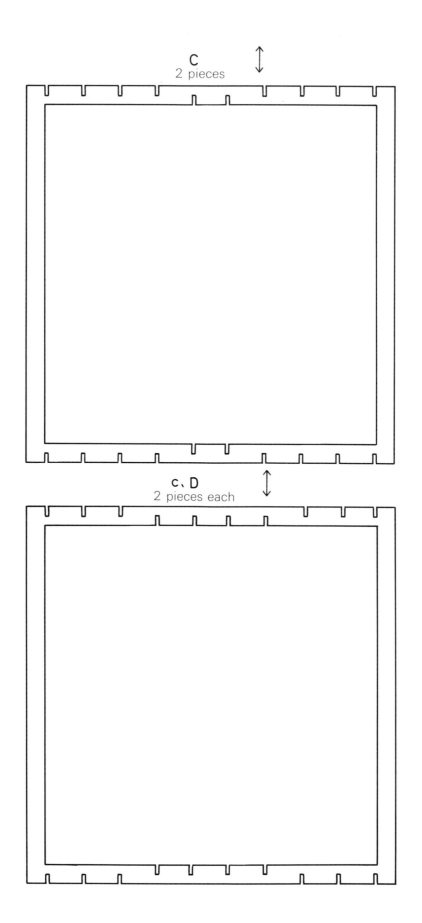

C
2 pieces

c、D
2 pieces each

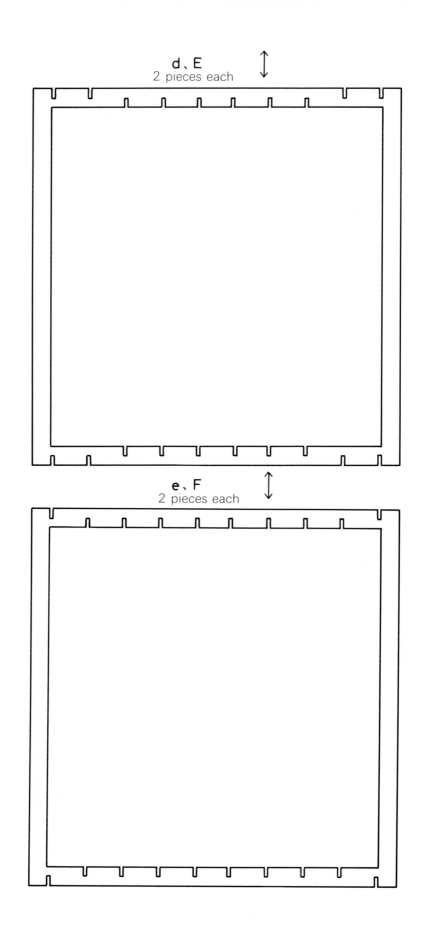

d、E
2 pieces each

e、F
2 pieces each

f
2 pieces

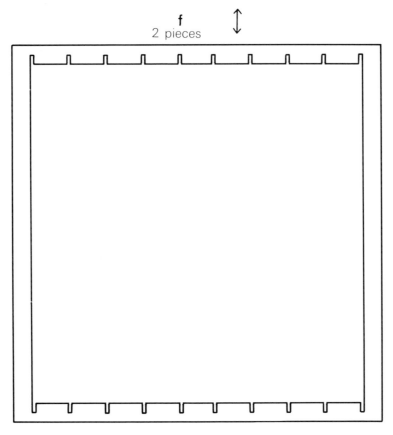

F E D C A A C D E F

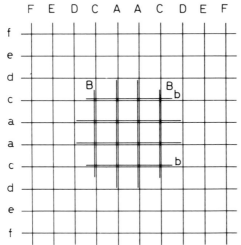

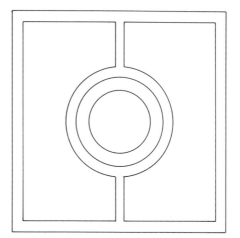

㊳ CRYSTAL CARD (HEXAHEDRON)
(shown on page 20)

Materials
3 Sheets white Bristol paper 15cm x 20cm (6″ × 8″)
(1 sheet for parts, 2 pieces for base)
1 Sheet colored Bristol paper 15cm x 20cm (6″ × 8″)
Japanese rice paper small piece
Thread small piece

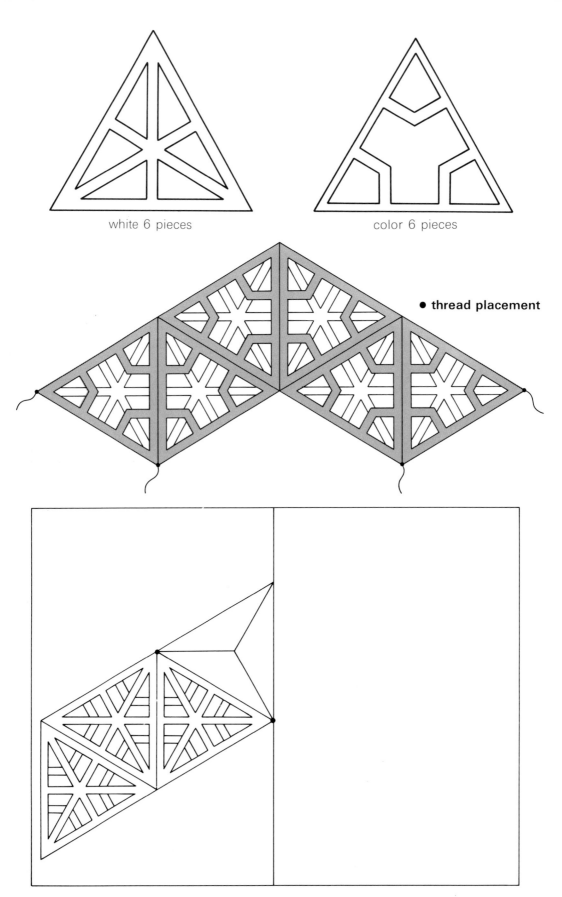

white 6 pieces

color 6 pieces

● **thread placement**

㉚ MYSTERY BOX (shown on page 16)

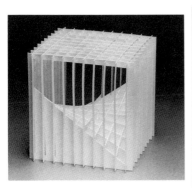

Materials
7 Sheets white Bristol paper
15cm x 20cm (6″ × 8″)

POINT
Be careful of paper grain
Arrows show grain direction

A
2 pieces

a
2 pieces

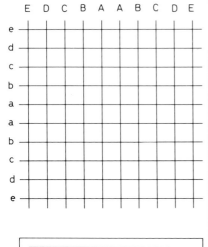

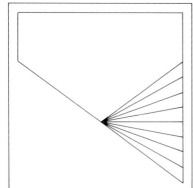

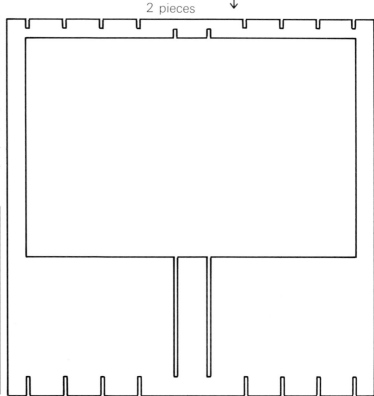

B
2 pieces

b
2 pieces

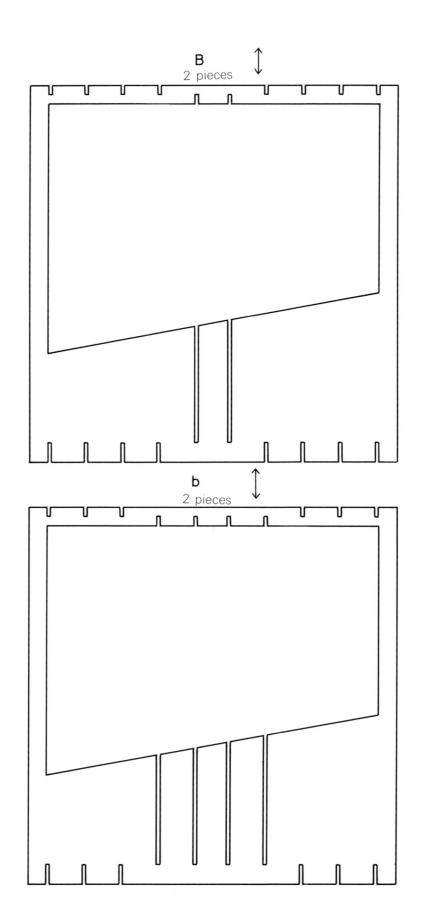

C
2 pieces

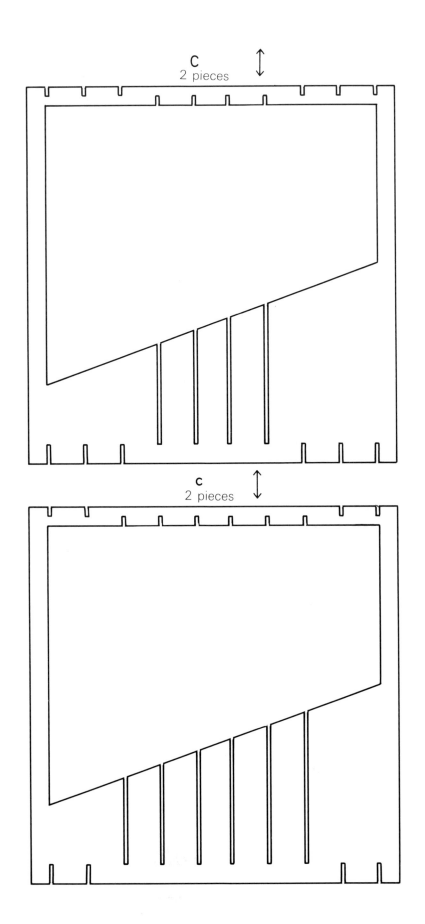

c
2 pieces

D
2 pieces

d
2 pieces

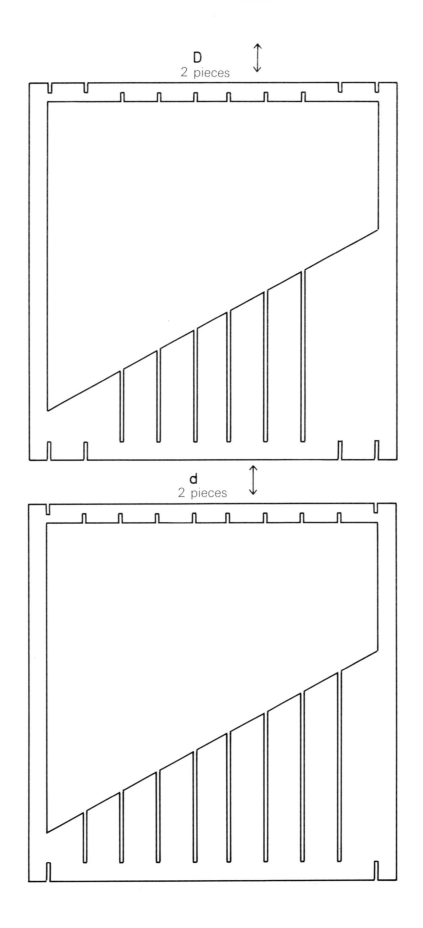

E
2 pieces

e
2 pieces

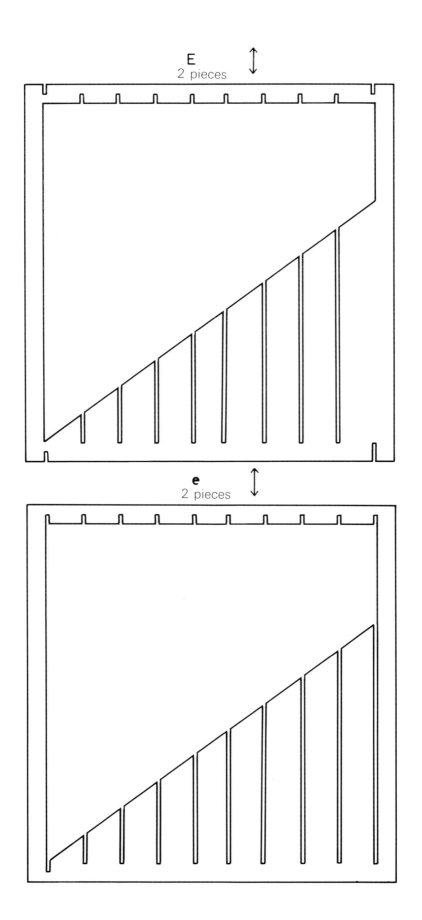

㉛ **MYSTERY BOX** (shown on page 17)

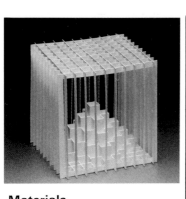

A 2 pieces ↕

Materials
7 Sheets white Bristol paper
15cm x 20cm (6″ × 8″)

POINT
Be careful of paper grain
Arrows show grain direction

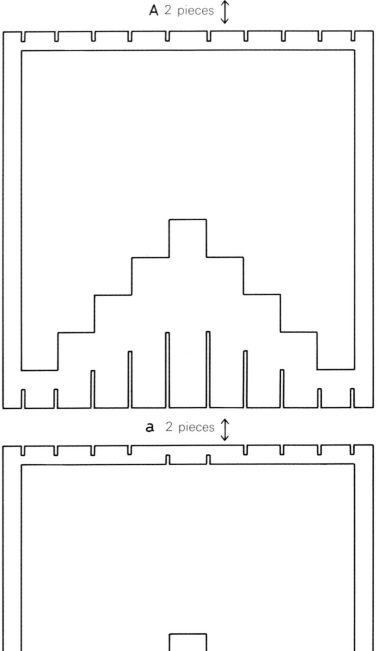

E D C B A A B C D E

e
d
c
b
a
a
b
c
d
e

a 2 pieces ↕

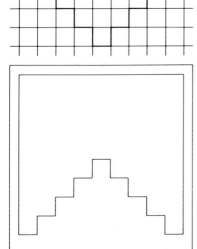

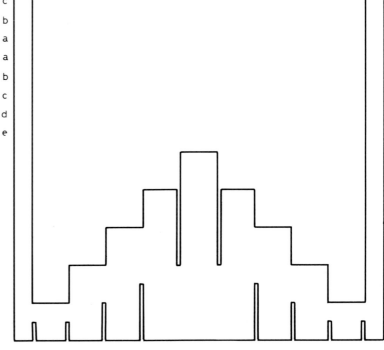

B   2 pieces ↕

b   2 pieces ↕

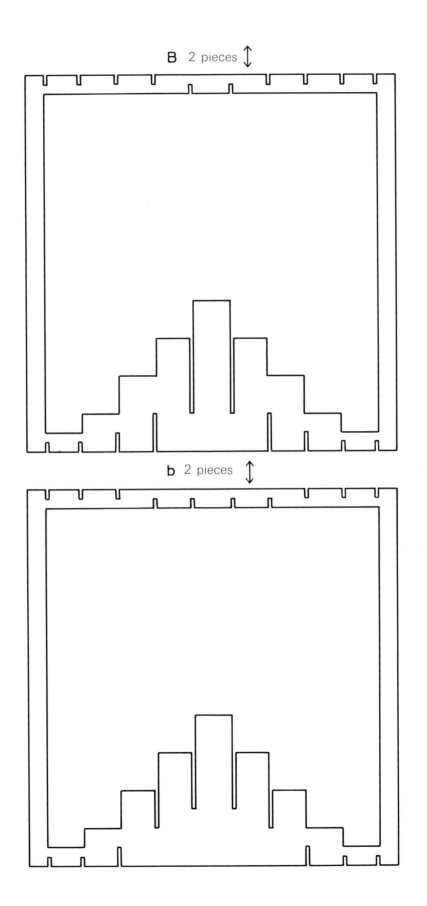

C   2 pieces

c   2 pieces

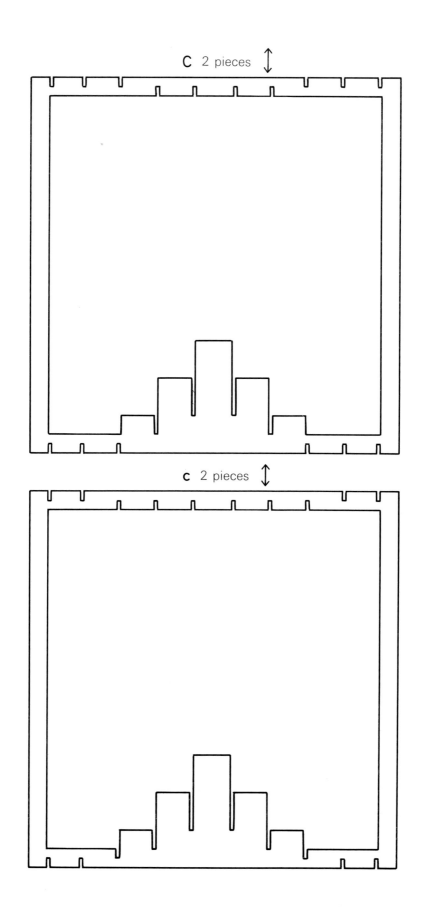

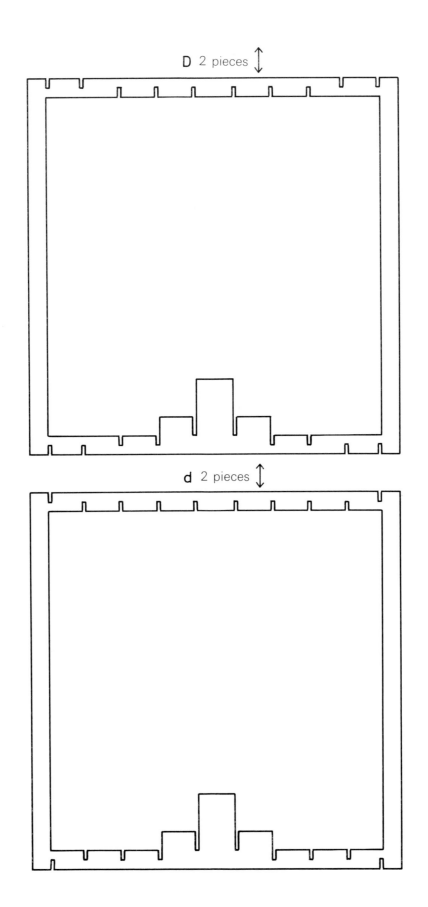

E 2 pieces

e 2 pieces

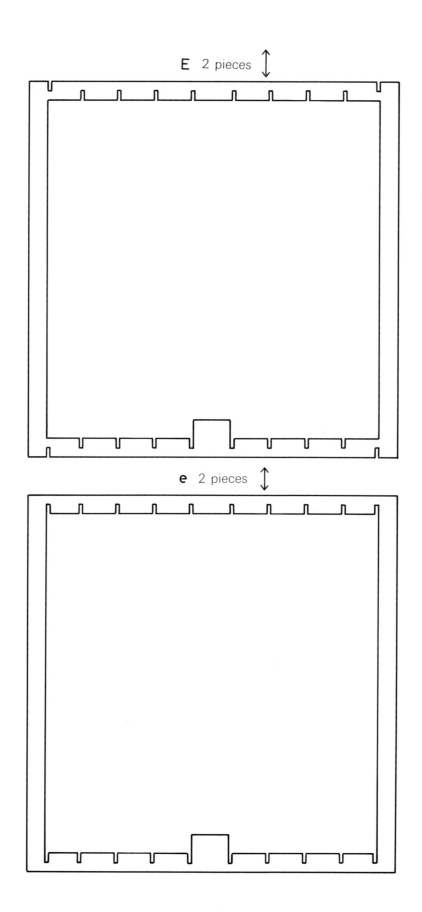

㉝ LOOP (shown on page 18)

Materials
2 Sheets two-colored construction paper
15cm x 20cm (6″ × 8″)

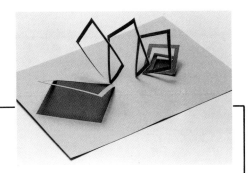

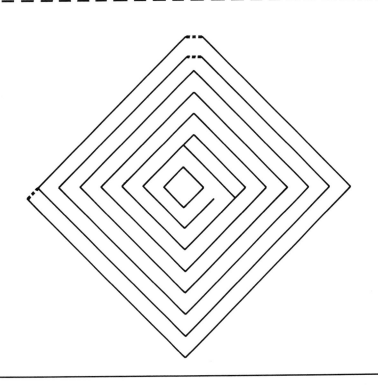

㉞ LOOP (shown on page 18)

Materials
2 Sheets two-colored construction paper
15cm x 20cm (6″ × 8″)

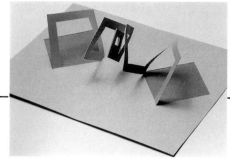

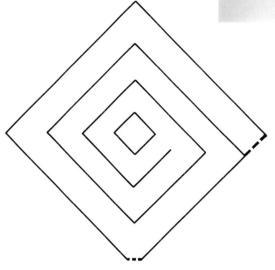

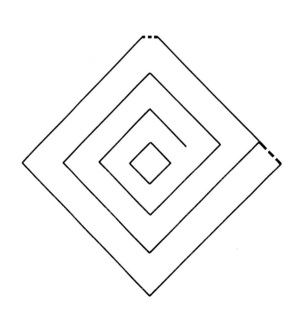

㊱ **LOOP** (shown on page 19)

Materials
2 Sheets two-colored construction paper
15cm x 20cm (6″ × 8″)

㉙ SUZHOU PRINCE REGENT'S PALACE
(shown on page 15)

Materials
4 Sheets white Bristol paper 15cm x 20cm (6″ × 8″)
(2 Sheets for parts, 2 Sheets for base)
Japanese rice paper small piece
Thread small piece

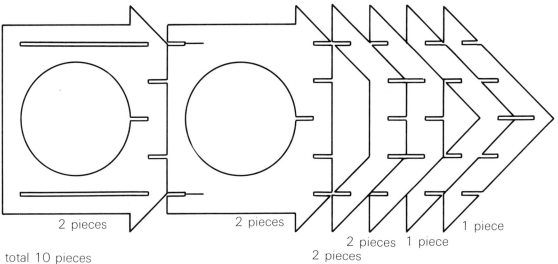

2 pieces

2 pieces

2 pieces

2 pieces

1 piece

1 piece

total 10 pieces

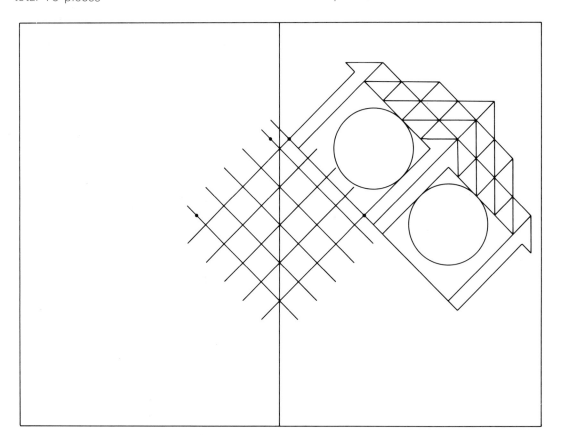

㉘ COMBINATION SHAPES
(shown on page 15)

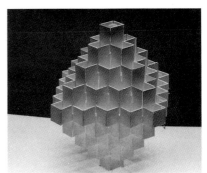

Materials
4 Sheets white Bristol paper 15cm x 20cm (6″ × 8″)
(2 sheets for parts, 2 sheets for base)
Japanese rice paper small piece
Thread small piece

Cut same pattern from 2 sheets of paper

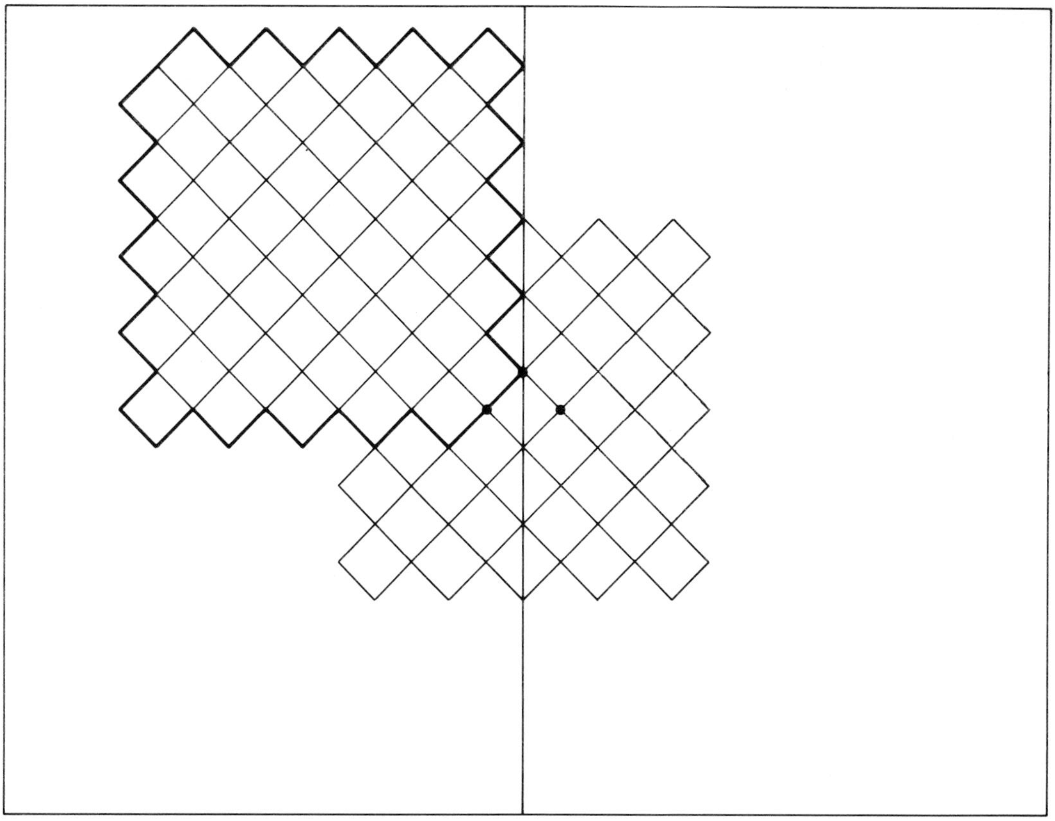

㊴ CRYSTAL CARD (OCTAHEDRON) (shown on page 20)

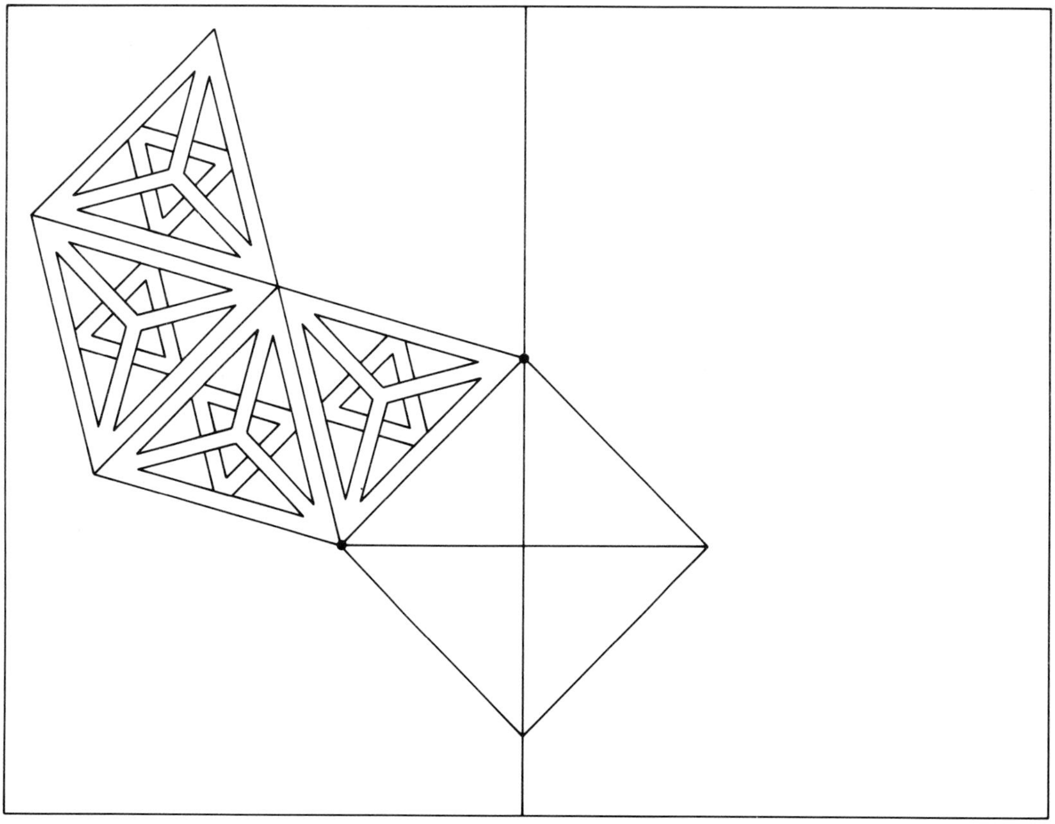

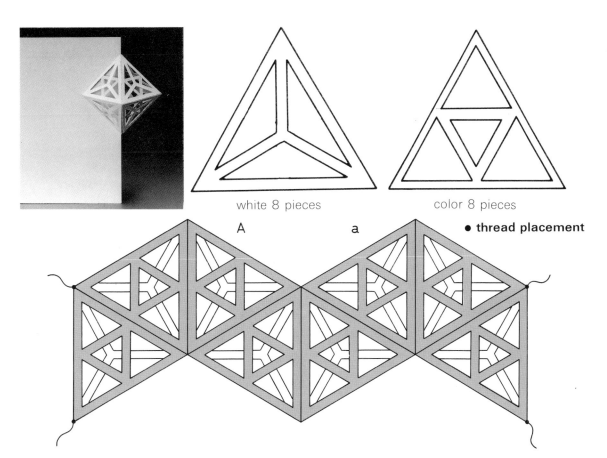

white 8 pieces

color 8 pieces

A   a   ● **thread placement**

㉖ **STADIUM** (shown on page 14)

Materials

3 Sheets white Bristol paper 15cm x 20cm (6" × 8") (1 sheet for parts, 2 sheets for base)

Japanese rice paper small piece   Thread small piece

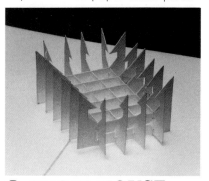

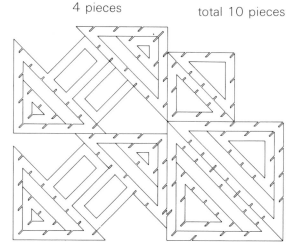

6 pieces

4 pieces   total 10 pieces

㉗ SNOW HOUSE
(shown on page 15)

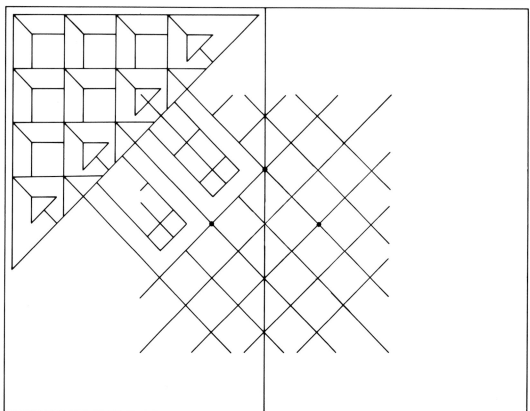

Materials

4 Sheets white Bristol paper
15cm x 20cm (6" × 8")
(2 sheets for parts, 2 sheets for base)
Japanese rice paper small piece
Thread small piece

※ If actual-size pattern is difficult
to trace, enlarge diagram from page 84
by three times.

A hobbyist's dream and a great gift, here's an enchanting world of paper pop-ups—the most novel origami books.

POP-UP ORIGAMIC ARCHITECTURE
by Masahiro Chatani

Open the finished cards and—pop!—out come animals, buildings, flowers, or intriguing abstract forms. The possibilities are endless, but author gives readers a solid start with complete instructions for thirty-eight designs. The actual cut-out patterns are given for twenty-four of them, making it easy to begin.

88 pages; 7¼" × 10¼"
A Paperback Original
ISBN 0-87040-656-6

POP-UP GREETING CARDS
by Masahiro Chatani

These delightful pop-up greeting cards—which anyone can have fun making with the simple instructions and ready-made cut-out patterns—were designed by an inventive architect whose handmade cards have been shown at the Museum of Modern Art. They're great for origami hobbyists or anyone who wants to give a truly attention-getting gift or greeting.

96 pages; 7¼" × 10¼"
A Paperback Original
ISBN 0-87040-733-3

POP-UP PAPER MAGIC
by Masahiro Chatani

A memorable business card is literally at your fingertips with this delightful new book of patterns from Masahiro Chatani, the architect who is a genius with cut and folded paper. Seventy different designs, including sports, flowers, birds, animals, and letters of the alphabet. All guaranteed to be memorable!

92 pages; 7¼" × 10¼"
A Paperback Original
ISBN 0-87040-757-0